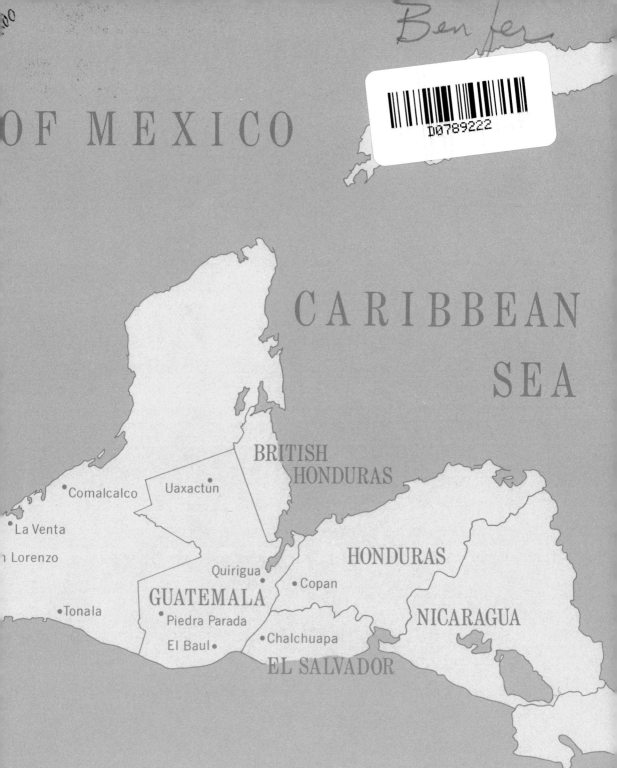

OF MEXICO

CARIBBEAN

SEA

• Comalcalco
Uaxactun•

BRITISH
HONDURAS

• La Venta

HONDURAS

n Lorenzo

Quirigua•
• Copan

•Tonala

GUATEMALA

NICARAGUA

• Piedra Parada

El Baul •

• Chalchuapa

EL SALVADOR

OCEAN

OLMEC

AN EARLY ART STYLE
OF PRE-COLUMBIAN MEXICO

AN EARLY ART STYLE

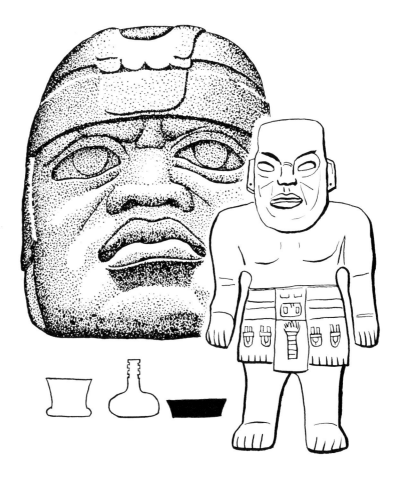

OLMEC

OF PRECOLUMBIAN MEXICO

Charles R. Wicke

THE UNIVERSITY OF ARIZONA PRESS
Tucson, Arizona

About the Author —

CHARLES R. WICKE's anthropological grasp of human societies enables him to bring alive the culture of the Olmec people through analysis of their art forms. During years of research devoted to comparing the fruits of Mesoamerican archaeology to their seeds in human history, Wicke has lived and worked in the geographic areas of his professional interest. From 1953 to 1961 he was a graduate student and instructor at the University of the Americas and carried out advanced studies at both the Escuela Nacional de Antropología e Historia and the Universidad Nacional Autónoma de México. Receiving the Ph.D. in anthropology from the University of Arizona in 1965, he returned to Mexico where he became co-chairman of the Department of Anthropology at the University of the Americas, leaving in 1966 for a Fulbright lectureship at the Universidad Nacional de Asunción in Paraguay. While in Paraguay he did ethnographic investigations of the Chulupí, an Indian group of the Chaco. He returned to the U.S. in 1968, first on the faculty of Northern Illinois University, later joining both the faculties of human ecology and anthropology at the University of Oklahoma. Wicke is the author of numerous articles on Mesoamerican antiquities and the translator of several Spanish language works on anthropology.

The title page drawing by the author
includes a Colossal Head from San Lorenzo, Veracruz,
a jadeite statue from the Tehuacan, Puebla, area,
and some Olmec ceramics.

THE UNIVERSITY OF ARIZONA PRESS

I.S.B.N.-0-8165-0185-8
L.C. No. 71-122581

For my parents

R. J. AND MARY

DEMCO

Contents

ILLUSTRATIONS

TABLES

Foreword

THE OLMECS, the most ancient civilized people in Mesoamerica, are the most recent to have come to our knowledge. Their name and everything about them are still a matter of divergent opinions — and probably will be for a long time to come. If today we command more information about them than anybody has ever had since the time of their fall more than two thousand years ago, we are yet sorely lacking proof for our very nice theories. Little do we know of their origin, their development, and their disappearance. Were it not for their sensational sculpture, they would pass unnoticed among the mass of Preclassic peoples, and their greatest feats — mathematical and calendrical — would still be ascribed to their brilliant heirs, the Maya. Thus any serious study that tries to lift even a corner of the veil of mystery is really welcome.

Charles Wicke came as a very young man to what was then Mexico City College, now the University of the Americas, as a graduate student in anthropology. As I was teaching there at the time, I knew him. My opinion of his work, talent and genuine interest has risen continuously in the ensuing span of time, as I have known him through his participation in excavations that I led and through his work in others that I simply visited.

Not only have I always liked the man himself, but also the way he works, the way he teaches, and the way he writes.

The very hard and frequently unrewarding life of teaching occasionally has its compensations. One of these rare moments comes when a former student "makes good" and brings out a book. It is still more pleasant when that book is important, well done, and controversial. I think this book is important because it deals, in a serious and scholarly manner, with an important people; it is well done because Wicke has gone into his subject deeply, weighed the different possibilities and arrived at some conclusions; and it is precisely this last factor which makes the book controversial — in a way that is scientific. This is a great asset.

This is not at all meant to recall the old and well-worn technique of *in cauda venenum*. Indeed, I am certain that my own hypotheses about this elusive and extraordinary people are as unconfirmed as I think Wicke's are, and I quite grant the possibility that he may be entirely right.

Wicke has analyzed two of the most striking products of these remote people — the Colossal Heads and the votive axes — in order to establish an order of appearance of each object of each type. The author's own sketches, drawings and photographs provide the reader with a view of this order. Thus this book is a study of evolution in Olmec art. The author's points are well taken though other possibilities exist. The same is true about his ideas on where this art originated. Covarrubias postulated Guerrero; Wicke now suggests northwestern Oaxaca; most scholars prefer southern Veracruz. The point is basic not only for Olmec history but for the understanding of Mesoamerica and even for a general concept about the birth of civilizations. Thus whatever the resultant controversy, Wicke's thesis will increase our basic knowledge.

IGNACIO BERNAL, *Director*
Museo Nacional de Antropología
México, D. F.

Preface

In 1956 Miguel Covarrubias gave a course at the Escuela
Nacional de Antropología e Historia in Mexico City. I was
fortunate enough to attend until classes were suspended because of a student strike. Up to the time of the strike we had
covered the Olmec, and Maestro Covarrubias's enthusiasm had
infected us all. I remember one particular occasion when I
had persuaded my friend Fernando Horcasitas to bring to class
a small yoke, purchased at Tlatilco, featuring a fierce Olmec
visage. Visibly excited by the piece, Covarrubias gloated, "Let
them deny an Olmec presence at Tlatilco after seeing that."
"Them" obviously referred to the U.S. Mayan scholars of the
Carnegie Institution, who blindly refused to see Olmec art as
coming before Maya.

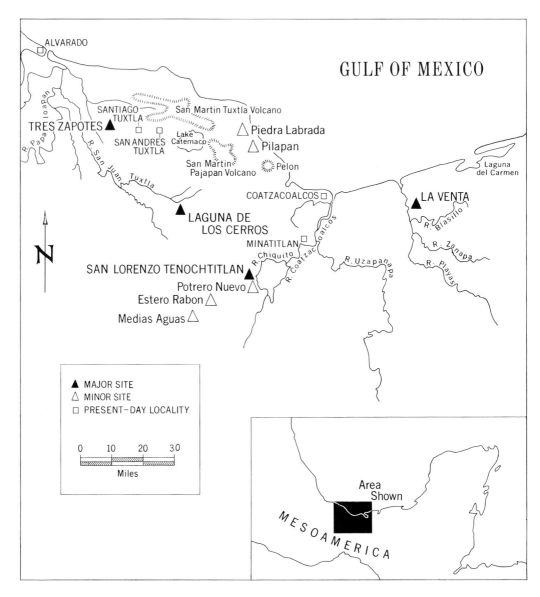

Fig. 1. Map of the Olmec heartland

In 1957, Miguel Covarrubias died. He left a superb collection of Precolumbian antiquities to the National Museum of Mexico, as well as many bright and happy murals, several beautifully illustrated books, and a multitude of saddened friends. Few men leave so much. Among his notes and papers was a chart on which were listed, across the top, 138 Olmec pieces from private and museum collections. In the lefthand margin were set down 89 stylistic elements such as eye-type or hand position. Within the matrix, the presence of each feature was marked with an X for each individual piece.

I did not know of the Covarrubias chart until 1962 when I ran across a copy while collecting materials for the present study. It seemed of great value just because of the information it contained. Later, I showed it to Jerry Miller of the sociology department of the University of Arizona with whom I was studying nonparametric statistics. He suggested that the data on the chart might lend themselves to Guttman scaling and referred me to the literature on the subject. Miller's advice proved to be of great utility; without it conclusions that I was able to reach would have been overlooked.

The purpose of this study has been to analyze the earliest great style of Precolumbian Mexico, the Olmec, in order to determine how it evolved and where it originated. Stone monuments with a stylistic unity which has come to be known as "Olmec" are found from northern Veracruz State to El Salvador (Endsheet map). Their heaviest concentration, however, is in the lowlands of the Mexican Gulf Coast between the Papaloapan and Tonalá rivers (Fig. 1). Here, massive sculpture was integrated into the architectural complexes thought by archaeologists to represent early ceremonial centers. The most famous and best explored of these is La Venta, a small island in northern Tabasco. Much of our solid knowledge about the creators of Olmec art has come from the patient explorations in the La Venta area by the late Frans Blom and Oliver La Farge and by Matthew Stirling, C. W. Weiant, Philip Drucker, and Robert Heizer, among others. It is a pleasure to acknowledge an obvious debt to them.

Olmec sculpture is also found scattered in museum collections. In trying to see as many of these as possible I was graciously received by the following persons: Ross Parmenter, my host and guide in New York City; Frederick Dockstader, director, Museum of the American Indian, Heye Foundation; Gordon Ekholm of the American Museum of Natural History; Clifford Evans of the U.S. National Museum; Miss Julie Jones of the Museum of Primitive Art; Professor Alfonso Medellín Z. of the Museum of Jalapa, Veracruz; Carlos Pellicer, Museo de Villahermosa, Tabasco; Professor Arturo Romano, former director, Museo Nacional de Antropología e Historia, México, D.F.; and Robert Wauchope, director, Museum of Middle American Research Institute of Tulane University.

For furnishing me with manuscripts of his prolific and stimulating Olmec studies before they appeared in print, I wish to thank Michael Coe of Yale University. For keeping me abreast of their exciting work on scale analysis, I am grateful to Robert L. Carneiro of the American Museum of Natural History and to Ward H. Goodenough of the University of Pennsylvania. C. W. Weiant was kind enough to answer a particular query. Professor Pal Keleman, author of *Medieval American Art*, gave wise counsel and warm encouragement. To Professor John Paddock, my colleague at the University of the Americas, I owe special thanks for seeing that my teaching assignments were covered during my absence from Mexico City and for sending me a photograph by Román Piña Chan of the Huamelulpan monolith, which proved to be invaluable for my researches. The financial aid of the U.S. Steel Foundation is recognized with appreciation.

Staff members of the Department of Anthropology, University of Arizona, where this study was done, have gone far beyond the requirements of their positions in extending succor and solace. Frederick Pleasants gamely suffered as my sounding board on many occasions. Professor Clara Lee Tanner's careful reading of the manuscript was evident from her penetrating questions which often led to helpful refinements. Emil Haury, department head during my stay, helped me over many a financial and academic hurdle; his personal warmth and his professionalism in archaeology have been great inspiration. Raymond Thompson, present department head, served as my advisor in the development of the dissertation that was the groundwork for this volume. Because of his highly developed sensitivity to wrong phrase or reference, he has agonized over my writing almost more than I. To me his editorial abilities remain a constant and delightful source of amazement. I appreciate as well the efforts of the University of Arizona Press staff in bringing about publication.

C.R.W.

OLMEC

AN EARLY ART STYLE
OF PRE-COLUMBIAN MEXICO

Understanding of culture as something more than an endless series of haphazard items is going to be achieved largely through recognition of patterns and our ability to analyze them.

A. L. KROEBER

1

History of the Olmec Problem

"As a work of art it is without exaggeration a magnificent sculpture," wrote the traveler to Veracruz, Mexico, José Melgar. The year was 1862. The magnificent sculpture was the first monumental Olmec sculpture to be discovered: the Colossal Head of Tres Zapotes. Thus begins the story of the "Olmec problem."

At first the head appeared to be the bottom of an inverted iron kettle projecting slightly above the rainforest bed. When peons from the nearby sugar plantation of Hueyapan set to digging, they exposed not a kettle, but a six-foot-tall basalt face of a giant. To Melgar its thick, grimly set lips and wide flat nose were African; this could only mean that the Gulf Coast of Mexico had once witnessed colonization from Ethiopia.

Fig. 2. Monument C, Tres Zapotes, Veracruz

Melgar's idea of African origins for the Colossal Head found support from others. Alfred Chavero was one of these. Lawyer, poet, governor of Mexico's Federal District, and author of eighteen theatrical works, Chavero had somehow found time to become the leading authority of his day on ancient Mexican history. In the encyclopedic work, *México a través de los siglos*, Chavero published in 1887 an engraving of the Colossal Head from Tres Zapotes to support Melgar's theory. As additional proof, he illustrated a large granite axe, now in New York's Museum of the American Indian (Fig. 34). In pointing out that the face sculptured on the axe strikingly duplicates the Tres Zapotes find in headdress and physical features, Chavero was the first to hint that the giant head was not an isolated phenomenon, but part of a complex. Like Melgar, he did not mention the term "Olmec."

Others did speak of the Olmecs at the close of the nineteenth century. In 1885 the Geographical Society of Paris published a note *"Opinion au sujet des Olmèques"* by M. Alphonse Pinart. Pinart identified the Olmecs as the Tepehuas of the eastern slope of the Sierra Madre Oriental where the states Veracruz, Hidalgo, and Puebla come together. In visiting the Tepehaus, he discovered they called their language "Ulmeca."

The question of Olmec identity arose at this time as a consequence of the first widespread publication of the sixteenth-century chroniclers, many of whom mentioned the Olmecs. One, Franciscan Father Bernardino de Sahagún (1961: vol. 10, 187–88), wrote of the Olmecs:

These, all of these, all were the people from the east. They were also named Tenime, because they spoke a barbarous tongue. These, according to the tradition were Tolteca—a branch, a remnant, of the Tolteca. These were rich; their home, their land, was really a land of riches, a land of flowers, a land of wealth, a land of abundance. There was all manner of food; there grew the cacao bean, and the "divine ear" spice, and wild cacao, and liquid rubber. There the magnolia and all different kinds of flowers grew. And there were the beautiful feathers, the precious feathers, [the feathers of] the troupial, the red spoonbill, the blue cotinga, the white-fronted parrot, the Mexican parrotlets; the resplendent trogonorus was also there. Also green stones, fine turquoise were found there. Also gold, silver were found there. It was a good, a beautiful place. The old people gave it the name Tlalocan, which is to say, "place of wealth."

Early Finds

Eduard Seler, a German investigator of Sahagún's works, showed more insight than Pinart in discussing the "Olmeca Uixtotin." In 1906, he noted that sixteenth-century sources labeled them inhabitants of the southern parts of the Gulf Coast who came originally from the Tlaxcala region. Seler (1906) attributed to these people certain monuments from the area of Tuxpan, Veracruz — monuments which would not fit into the Olmec style as defined today. Nevertheless, he was the first scholar seeking to associate an art style with the Olmecs. The trend set by Seler is important to our story.

Seler and his wife visited the Tres Zapotes region in 1905 and photographed the Colossal Head and the elaborately carved stone box now called Monument C (Fig. 2). In the account of the trip (Seler-Sachs 1922: 544), Mrs. Seler attributed these monuments to no group. She said only that the head doubtless was not attached to a body, and likened it to a smaller solitary head from Mexico City of the Aztec Moon Goddess Coyolxauhqui. The Tres Zapotes head, however, seemed not to depict a specific god, but rather was a portrait.

The year 1907 gave the world notice of another important find from the area of the Colossal Head. W. H. Holmes (1907), curator of the Smithsonian Institution, published a description of a remarkable figurine (Fig. 3), a winged, duck-billed personage closely related in style to the Olmec.

"A nephrite statuette from San Andres Tuxtla, Vera Cruz" relates an intriguing tale of discovery. In June 1902, Holmes had received a letter from one Alfred Bishop Mason in Orizaba, Veracruz: "I send you herewith two photographs of a jade idol which was dug up by the plow in the district of San Andres Tuxtla on the Gulf Coast . . . ." Then, in July of the following year, a letter postmarked New York reached Holmes from R. E. Ulbricht who had brought the statuette from Veracruz: "If this should be of interest to you for the purpose of deciphering the hieroglyphs or to acquire it for the collection in the Smithsonian Institution, please advise me and I will take pleasure in sending it to you by express."

Thus, without leaving Washington, Holmes had the fantastic luck of acquiring through two courtly correspondents — total strangers, apparently — the most fascinating figurine to come from Mesoamerica.

The publication did credit to the find. Holmes, who ended his government career as director of the National Gallery of Art, had studied drawing and produced never-surpassed illustrations of Mesoamerican ruins. He was one to appreciate the aesthetic value of the Tuxtla Statuette. Yet he did not neglect its scientific value; he included photographs and drawings clearly depicting the hieroglyphs covering the figurine (Fig. 4).

Fig. 3. Winged duckbill — the Tuxtla Statuette

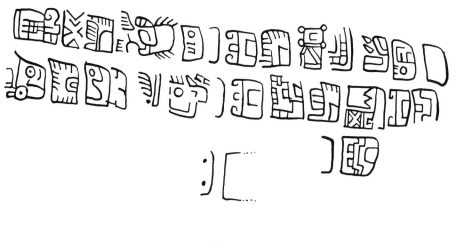

Fig. 4. Glyphs from the Tuxtla Statuette

Commentaries on the glyphs were solicited from Maya specialists. Although the 6½-inch Tuxtla Statuette bears a date in the so-called "Maya" system, it seemed earlier than any date found in the Maya area to the south. The bar-and-dot numbers (Fig. 4, second row) incised down the front of the figurine carry a Long Count date of 8.6.2.4.17. If, indeed, it follows the same system with the same starting point as the Maya used, the date on the Tuxtla Statuette is A. D. 162, using the generally followed Goodman-Martínez-Thompson correlation. Michael Coe (1962: 62) classifies the statuette stylistically as "epi-Olmec." The historical significance of the figurine lies in its falling stylistically and temporally between the earlier Olmec and the later Maya cultural remains.

In 1924 an even earlier date came to light about 400 air miles southwest from the Tuxtla region. On a hacienda called El Baul near the Pacific coast of Guatemala, T. T. Waterman encountered a large stela. The massive monument bears a standing figure with an elaborately voluted headdress. The figure faces two columns of badly worn glyphs. Painstakingly, Waterman traced these shallow reliefs in charcoal prior to photographing them. When the results of his efforts were published, they were, to use Waterman's words, "appropriated in a way" by the German investigator Walter Lehmann. Actually all Lehmann did was to note that the glyphs include a column of bar-and-dot numbers that make up an Initial Series date. Just as on the Tuxtla Statuette, the numbers appear alone and lack the associated time-period glyphs shown by all Initial Series attributed to the Maya. The first number clearly reads as a seven, placing the date within the seventh cycle or before A. D. 62 in the GMT correlation. Lehmann's reading (1926: 175, f.n. 4) was 7.19.7.6.12 12 Eb, 20 Kankin.

Waterman (1929) attacked this view. The sign of a mandible, which Lehmann had read as the Maya day sign Eb, could only be a glyph used exclusively by the Aztecs: a sign for the earth monster. Therefore, the monument had to be an Aztec copy of a Maya stela.

Fig. 5. Stela 1, La Venta

M. Coe (1957: 600-3) has convincingly refuted this idea. His slight correction of Lehmann's reading leaves us with 7.19.15.7.12 12 Eb, or A. D. 36 using the GMT correlation. The date appears appropriate on stylistic grounds. The headdress is reminiscent of other late Olmec or Olmecoid reliefs – particularly those at Chalcatzingo – in its volutes and the bearded human profile contained within them.

The Discovery of La Venta

Franz Blom and Oliver La Farge hit upon a second Colossal Head in 1925. Danish archaeologist Blom and twenty-four-year-old La Farge sailed from New Orleans on February 19, 1925, as the two-man "Tulane Expedition to Middle America." La Farge had been graduated the year before from Harvard where he edited the *Lampoon*. Behind him lay three seasons of archaeological fieldwork in Arizona. The veteran Blom was the expedition's archaeologist, however; La Farge its ethnologist.

Exploring southeastern Mexico, Blom and La Farge climbed the San Martín Pajapan volcano. Here a magnificent idol of purest Olmec style awaited them (Blom and La Farge 1926: Fig. 43m p. 47). Because it obviously was not Maya, Totonac, Aztec, or any other then-familiar style, they could "not venture to ascribe it definitely to any culture" (p. 46).

The two guided themselves in part by the narrative of the Spanish conquistador, Bernal Díaz del Castillo. Cortez's companion had described a populated town about one league from the mouth of the Tonalá River. On reaching this location, the explorers indeed found ruins. However, these ruins could not have been of the settlement described by Bernal Díaz. Today we know that at the time of Spanish Conquest the site had been long abandoned. What Blom and La Farge had discovered proved to be the Olmec site *par excellence:* La Venta, Tabasco (Fig. 5).

At La Venta, the explorers cleared and photographed a half-dozen stone sculptures. "The most amazing monument of them all" was the second Colossal Head to be discovered. They noted its resemblance to the one from Tres Zapotes. Yet, because of its massiveness, they were unable to excavate it and could observe only the exposed part down to eye level (Fig. 6).

Although the style of the monuments at La Venta patently was not Maya, Blom and La Farge foreshadowed some of my own views in pointing out certain similarities of the new style to that of the Maya. In Stela 2 (Fig. 7) they saw Maya influence in the elaborate headdress and diagonally held ceremonial bar of the central figure. Altar 4 (Fig. 8) demonstrated a "strong Maya feeling" in that "the person in the niche resembles figures on Stela E at Piedras Negras," the Maya site on the Guatemala side of the Usumacinta River.

The two also called attention to a problem that has intrigued later archaeologists — Heizer (Heizer and Williams 1960) in particular — the source of igneous stone for the alluvial zone. Petroleum geologist N. F. Keller told them that blocks could have been brought to the island site of La Venta from outcrops 60 miles upriver at La Laja.

Ill luck was to visit Blom and La Farge. Much of the film exposed at La Venta came out blank. Fortunately, the monuments were photographed a few years later by an English hunter, H. A. Knox, and published in the British journal *Man* (Joyce and Knox 1931).

La Venta's monuments, in a hitherto unknown style, caused Blom and La Farge to judge the site as "certainly a place of many puzzles."

The story of the discovery of La Venta does not end with the publication of Blom and La Farge's final report. In a review of the book which resulted from their explorations, Herman Beyer (1927) published an "Olmecan idol." Its features reminded Beyer of those on the jaguar mask set in the headdress of Blom and La Farge's San Martín Pajapan statue: slanted eyes, broad, flat nose, downturned feline mouth. The "Olmecan

Fig. 6. Top of Colossal Head, La Venta

idol" (Fig. 33) was an axe similar to that which Chavero had published in 1887.

Nevertheless, we cannot credit Beyer with assigning the name to the style. In the end he equivocated by saying the deity on the San Martín headdress pertained "to the Olmecan *or* Totonacan civilization" (italics added).

The Naming of the Style

Marshall H. Saville was a staff member of the Museum of the American Indian in New York City. It was here that the axe published by Chavero came to rest after a stay in Switzerland. The acquisition prompted Saville, a Mexican specialist, to write a comparative study of the known axes of this type. He also noted their stylistic resemblance to other forms: a jadeite

Fig. 7. Stela 2, La Venta

Fig. 8. Altar 4, La Venta

bead ornament, a figurine, a head, and an idol. These shared a common style and could be "safely assigned to the ancient Olmecan culture, which apparently had its center in the San Andrés Tuxtla area around Lake Catemaco, and extended down to the coast of the Gulf of Mexico in the southern part of the State of Vera Cruz" (Saville 1929: 285).

George C. Vaillant, of the American Museum of Natural History, concurred with Saville's view. Vaillant was a rare combination of scientific archaeologist and humanist. His published analyses of Aztec and Maya pieces show a deep appreciation of art and understanding of aesthetic principles. Noting that "we know the art styles of the Aztec, the Toltec, the Zapotec, perhaps the Totonac, and certainly the Maya" but not the creators of the art style which depicted jaguar faces and baby faces, he continued (1932: 519–20):

But there is often described in the traditions a highly civilized people called the Olmec, who lived anciently as far north as Tlazcala, but were later dispersed to southern Vera Cruz, Chiapas, southern Puebla, and eastern

[13]

Fig. 9a. Stela 3, La Venta

[14]

Fig. 9b. Detail of Stela 3

Oaxaca. They were famed for their work in jade and turquoise, and were credited with being the chief users of rubber in Central America.

The geographical position of these people roughly coincides with the distribution of the "tiger-face" and "baby-face" sculptures and they could have been in contact with Nahua tribes to the north, Zapotec to the west, the central Maya to the southwest, and the Maya and Mexican populations of Yucatan to the southeast. However, no material culture has been assigned to these Olmec.

Thus in view of an art style which is foreign to the defined civilizations, a geographical situation roughly coterminous with the centers of distribution of the art styles, and a historical position which is relatively early, it would seem that the Olmec fulfill very well the requirements for the peculiar art styles we have been discussing. Moreover, Professor Saville in his paper on "Votive Axes" lends his authority to the suggestion.

Vaillant recognized that since no scientific excavations had been carried out in the Olmec area, his hypothesis was at best impressionistic. To strengthen it, he urged a program of exploratory work in the area. In 1932 the Bureau of American Ethnology of the Smithsonian Institution formulated a plan to study archaeologically the margins of the Maya zone.

Chalcatzingo

The archaeologist Eulalia Guzmán is today famous in Mexico as the "discoverer" of the bones of her country's last Aztec emperor, Cuauhtémoc, at Ixcateopan in western Morelos. Back in 1934, however, Miss Guzmán was an earnest young student intrepidly exploring the *terra incognita* of eastern Morelos on horseback. In March of that year she discovered near Jonacatepec the only Olmec carvings known from central Mexico: the Chalcatzingo reliefs (Figs. 10, 11, 12).

One of the reliefs shows a solitary personage seated upon a box-like throne within what appears to be a cave (Fig. 10). The headdress and the horizontally held bar remind us of the same garb from the Olmec heartland site of La Venta (Figs. 7, 9). The volutes, which may represent smoke pouring from the cave, are shaped like those of the headdress on the El Baul stela.

Fig. 10. The Chalcatzingo reliefs

Figs. 11, 12. The Chalcatzingo reliefs and detail (below)

Fig. 13. Relief from Actopan, Veracruz

A second scene (Fig. 11) obviously indicates a ceremony. Three standing figures wear La Venta-like headdresses and jaguar masks. While two of them may carry maces, the one on the left supports a maize plant as does a figure on the recently discovered relief from Actopan in northern Veracruz (Fig. 13). The naked and bearded individual leans against a jaguar masked idol. Bound at the wrists, he seemingly is about to become a sacrificial victim. His sex is depicted — an exceptional departure for an Olmec artist.

Just as Blom and La Farge before her at La Venta, Guzmán (1934: 251) failed to pinpoint the style: "Not being Aztec representations, they can be those of some of the cultural groups that inhabited what is today the state of Morelos, the Teotihuacanos, or the Archaics" [translation mine].

[19]

The Role of the National Geographic Society

The Bureau of Ethnology program of explorations conceived by Vaillant focused on the area west of the Maya by 1938. Early that year, Matthew W. Stirling, director of the Bureau, visited southern Veracruz. Guided by the published accounts, he located the Colossal Head at Tres Zapotes, cleared the earth from its face, and carried photographs of it back to Washington. With these he convinced the officers of the wealthy National Geographic Society that archaeological research in the area merited their support.

Stirling returned to Tres Zapotes on January 2 of the following year as leader of the "National Geographic Society-Smithsonian Institution Expedition to Vera Cruz." His first task was to uncover the giant head. Twenty men did the job in two

Fig. 14. Glyphs on Stela C, Tres Zapotes

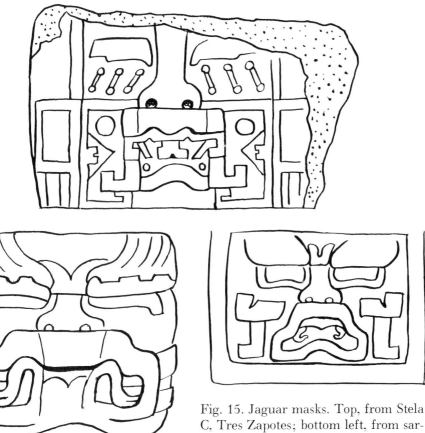

Fig. 15. Jaguar masks. Top, from Stela C, Tres Zapotes; bottom left, from sarcophagus, La Venta; bottom right, from Monument 15, La Venta.

days. The head rested on a prepared flagstone surface. Another sculpture, Stela A, originally about eighteen feet high, was found in two pieces, apparently intentionally broken (Stirling 1943a: 13). The magnificently carved box, Monument C (Fig. 2), originally described by the Selers, was excavated once more.

On January 16, 1939, Stirling made a truly revolutionary discovery. At the base of the largest mound at Tres Zapotes the corner of a worked stone projected inches above ground. Unearthing it, Stirling found a vertical row of bar-and-dot numbers apparently forming a date (Fig. 14). On the well-worn opposite side snarls a highly stylized jaguar mask of Olmec tradition (Fig. 15). As on the Tuxtla Statuette and on the El Baul stela, the numbers lacked glyphs designating time periods.

Like other Tres Zapotes monuments, this one had been broken. The break occurred so as to leave no *baktun* or cycle number. Nevertheless, a day sign with its coefficient 6 remained. Within this context only a baktun reading of 7 could be compatible with the day number. Stirling's reading of the monument, Stela C, was (7).16.6.16.18, 6 Eznab 1 Uo, 31 B.C. in the Goodman-Martínez-Thompson correlation, or 291 B.C. in the Spinden correlation. Perhaps encouraged by the *National Geographic* editors, Stirling picked the earlier 291 B.C. date for the feature article "Discovering the New World's Oldest Dated Work of Man."

Mayan scholars attacked Stirling's reading of Stela C. Morley (1946: 41) and Thompson (1941: 14-15) had credited the Maya with the invention of the Mesoamerican calendar and numerical system. After a lifetime of research on the Maya, they understandably felt a certain loyalty to them. It was inconceivable, therefore, that a "Mayan" date should appear outside the Maya area earlier than any within it.

Despite the initial outcries, Stirling's reading has been upheld. The radiocarbon method for dating, developed since, has supported the placement of Stela C within cycle 7 (Coe 1957: 598–99). The authoritative epigrapher who first opposed Stirling's reading, J. Eric Thompson (1954: 50), has admitted the possibility of its correctness.

It is no less than amazing that just enough information was left on the broken stela to permit a reading. Stirling (1939: 216) did not exaggerate: "If three inches more had been broken off either the top or the bottom of the monument, the date never could have been determined."

La Venta Revisited

During the 1940 season Stirling acted with assurance. Quite logically, he followed the footsteps of Blom and La Farge. They had reported a Colossal Head at La Venta; Stirling wished

Fig. 16. Altar 5, La Venta

to compare the Tres Zapotes Colossal Head with it. Not only
was he able to locate it and five other known monuments, he
discovered fourteen new pieces. The serene Altar 5 (Fig. 16)
was one of these.

The most surprising finds, however, were three additional
Colossal Heads! Stirling uncovered them one by one in a row
facing away from the site at its northern limits (Map, Fig. 17,
and Fig. 18). Thus he obtained four times the comparative
material that he had originally sought.

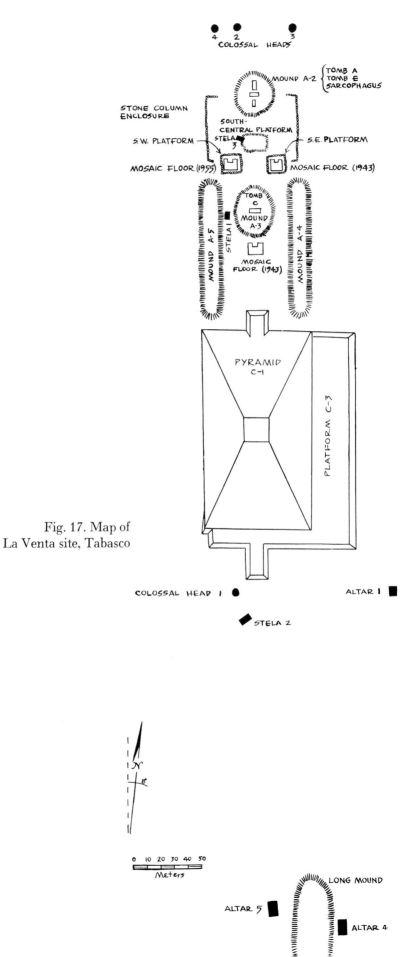

Fig. 17. Map of
La Venta site, Tabasco

Fig. 18. Altar 2, La Venta

Superb photographs of the La Venta monoliths glowed from the pages of the September, 1940, issue of *National Geographic Magazine*. The sculptors of the pieces were called "Olmecs" in the *Geographic* story. Thus, for the first time La Venta and the Olmecs hit the public eye. The impact of the article in the widely circulated magazine guaranteed Stirling the financial backing of the *Geographic* in future years.

The success of Stirling's strategy was matched by the failure of his tactics. His sense of *where* to look was uncanny, his sense of *how* to look unconcerned. His field methods — or rather the lack of them — seem anachronistic in mid-twentieth century. Stirling's procedures seemed patterned more to the previous century of Heinrich Schliemann and Flinders Petrie than to those of scientific archaeology. Avarice for museum pieces often blinded the nineteenth-century explorers to archaeological contexts. Despite an uninhibited and freewheeling approach, the archaeologists of the pre-scientific era made discoveries that their cautious counterparts of today might miss.

The same may be said of Stirling. In the 1940 season, for example, he spent a mere ten days unearthing and photographing the monumental sculpture at La Venta. No time was wasted in determining the archaeological context of the pieces: their associations with geological or ceramic strata.

Yet Stirling dared an undertaking of which others had been timorous. He opened a whole new world to Mexican archaeology. Perhaps the only approach that could have succeeded was a bold and brash one. This, in turn, resulted in the *National Geographic's* generous, long-term financial support, without which ballast an archaeologist is a captain without a ship. Furthermore, through crisp reproduction, the *Geographic* introduced La Venta monuments to a wide audience.

It is also to Stirling's credit that, although indifferent himself to the problems of context and stratigraphy, he did employ an assistant to deal with the more mundane aspects of excavation. Stirling's associate for the 1939 season had been W. C. Weiant, a chiropractor turned archaeologist. Weiant had been attracted to archaeology while practicing his original profession in Zamora, Michoacán, Mexico, in the mid-1920s. He took a degree in anthropology at Columbia University in 1937. Each summer he returned to Mexico where he worked under Mexican archaeologist Alfonso Caso. He also studied Mexican material at museums in the eastern United States, including, under Vaillant, the Saville collection at the American Museum of Natural History.

Weiant (1952: 58), with a broad knowledge of Mexican artifacts, was nonetheless deficient in field experience. Eschewing stratigraphic excavations at Tres Zapotes, he collected ceramic materials that were dug up in mound explorations, grave lots, or incidental to Stirling's excavations for large stone sculpture. In his report, Weiant (1943) arranged the material stylistically and noted outside influences upon it. For economic reasons, he returned to chiropractic after the field season.

Archaeologist Philip Drucker, a cowboy in his youth, took over as Stirling's assistant the following season, 1940. In contrast to Weiant, he was familiar with field techniques, but lacked knowledge of Mesoamerican ceramics (Drucker 1952: 259). Since receiving his doctorate from the University of California in 1936, he had worked almost exclusively with the ethnology and archaeology of the Northwest Coast Indians. At Tres Zapotes Drucker concentrated on controlled stratigraphic excavation by digging his pits away from mound structures. Thus his columns of sherds, accumulated throughout the occupation of the site, would represent undisturbed layers.

Given their difference of approach, it is understandable that Weiant's and Drucker's results did not coincide. In itself, this perhaps would have been unimportant except that the chronological position of La Venta soon became central to the Olmec problem. The single ceramic horizon at La Venta, to take on chronological significance, had to be fitted into the much longer sequence at nearby Tres Zapotes.

While Drucker excavated at Tres Zapotes in 1940, Stirling visited the Cerro de las Mesas site where he discovered twelve stelae and eight other monuments. The richness of his find influenced him to dig at the site during the following season.

Stirling's work at Cerro de las Mesas in 1940 and 1941 does not bear directly on the Olmec story. It is significant, however, that Initial Series dates without time period glyphs were dug up. They show the persistence of this manner of annotation in

the Gulf Coast region for at least a half-millennium after similar inscriptions were carved on the Tuxtla Statuette and on
Tres Zapotes Stela C.

Furthermore, on the last day at Cerro de las Mesas, a jade
cache was discovered in a spot that had been worn down by
wheelbarrow traffic. Being pressed for time, Stirling (1941:
292) had the 782 pieces removed within half an hour! Among
them glistened three Olmec heirlooms, all of blue jade: a canoe
with two incised Olmec profiles, a macaw pendant, and a
chubby dwarf.

The 1942 season saw Stirling once more at La Venta.
Philip Drucker joined him to study the ceramic stratigraphy
and thereby locate La Venta in time, relative to the Maya and
other Classic cultures. Among the spectacular finds of this
fourth field season was a burial chamber fashioned of basalt
columns in which "ancient bones reposed in a shroud of brilliant cinnabar amid masterpieces of the jade carver's art"
(Stirling and Stirling, 1942). In line with the crypt a few feet
away, a bathtub-shaped sarcophagus with a slab top and a tiger
mask was uncovered (Fig. 15).

More important to the resolution of the chronological
problem, however, were the many bags of pottery sherds which
Drucker collected and sent back to the Smithsonian Institution
in Washington. Drucker had planned to analyze them there on
his return from Mexico. But fate had other plans for him. The
U. S. was at war, and Drucker entered the Naval Reserve. He
did not see his sherds or field notes for three years (Drucker
1952: ix). Not until 1947 did his preliminary study appear.
Meanwhile the problem of La Venta chronology remained un-
resolved, though vehemently discussed.

The Views of Mexican Scholars

A storm of controversy had built up over interpretation of
the Olmec finds. Much argument arose from the dearth of
knowledge about La Venta stratigraphy, which, if known,

would give a relative chronology. Was the Olmec style late or early? Was it contemporary with the Maya or did it come before?

Sponsored by the Sociedad Mexicana de Antropología, a round table met at the end of summer 1942, at Tuxtla Gutiér-rez, Chiapas, to consider the Olmec question. Stirling, fresh from the field, reported on his jade discoveries from the basalt burial chamber at La Venta.

Trenchant debate characterized the sessions. At issue was the placement in time of the Olmec as well as its significance in the development of other Mesoamerican cultures. Mexican authorities, following Alfonso Caso, generally held that the Olmec was a "mother culture" flourishing before the Maya and other Classic cultures. North American scholars such as Thompson, Stirling, and Drucker favored a Classic date con-temporary with the Maya.

The holders of these irreconcilable views left the meetings unconvinced by the arguments of the opposition. The Ameri-cans generally could not understand how the sophisticated style of the Olmecs could be mother to the Maya. Did their studies not show the Maya culture arising in splendid isolation in the jungles of the Petén in Guatemala? The Mexicans could not comprehend how romantic loyalty to the Maya could so blind Americans to the facts.

A more positive result of the round table was a precise definition of the term "Olmec" in both its stylistic and histori-cal aspects. Amplifying his views expressed at Tuxtla Gutiérrez, the Mexican historian, Wigberto Jiménez Moreno, published his incisive "El Enigma de los Olmecas" in September, 1942. It indicated that the problem was complex; Jiménez (1942:145) came up with five varieties of Olmecs: *pre-*, *proto-*, *paleo-*, *neo-*, and *post*-Olmecs.

In its broadest sense, the term "Olmec" means "an inhabi-tant of the rubber region," that is, of southern Veracruz and northern Tabasco. Thus it could be applied to a succession of peoples who have lived in this zone. The Olmecs to whom the sixteenth-century chronicler Sahagún referred were but the most recent inhabitants of the area, whom Jiménez termed *post*-Olmecs. The creators of the monumental sculpture at La Venta were the earliest or *pre*-Olmecs. Between these fitted a succession of other groups which ancient Mexican historical sources labeled Olmec. The archaeological Olmecs were thought by Jiménez to be a Mayan people who spoke a Mayan language that was a precursor of present-day Huastec.

At the same meetings in Tuxtla Gutiérrez, the first comprehensive definition of Olmec style was put forward by Mexican artist Miguel Covarrubias, a definition that we shall consider further on. Covarrubias was well qualified to develop the analysis of style, having been a highly successful illustrator, mural painter, and set designer. Born in 1904 in Mexico City, he was a syndicated cartoonist at seventeen. He received a Mexican government fellowship for art study in New York in 1923. He drew caricatures for *Vanity Fair* and the *New Yorker*, designed sets for the 1925 production of Shaw's *Androcles and the Lion*, and did book illustrations *(New York Times*, Feb. 6, 1957: 26).

Covarrubias developed an interest in anthropology during two stays in Bali. His beautifully illustrated *Island of Bali* (1937) is more than a travel book; it is an ethnographical study. He displayed his general knowledge of Pacific ethnography in executing six giant mural maps with the theme "Pageant of the Pacific" for the San Fancisco International Exposition of 1939. When he turned his attention to the Isthmus of Tehuantepec in his own country, another delightful combination of art and anthropology resulted: the book *Mexico South* (1946). Here he illustrated many Olmec objects, reviewed the Olmec problem, and presented Jiménez Moreno's views to English readers. His posthumously published *Indian Art of Mexico and Central America* (1957: 50-83) gives the best summary of the Olmec available today. At Tuxtla Gutiérrez, Covarrubias aligned himself with those who held that La Venta culture came before Classic Maya.

The Drucker-Weiant Exchange

To illustrate the intensity of feeling generated by the Olmec problem, we have but to consider the Drucker-Weiant exchange. Drucker's report on Tres Zapotes ceramics appeared along with Weiant's in 1943. The Tres Zapotes sequence was important to the Olmec problem because it was much longer than, and apparently overlapped that at La Venta. Strangely enough, the two reports, although dealing with the same subject and written by men working for the Bureau of American Ethnology, differ markedly in presentation and periodification. Obviously the authors had not consulted each other.

Drucker (1943: 118-19) broke down Tres Zapotes ceramics into three phases: Lower, Middle, and Upper. In the Lower Tres Zapotes horizon, he observed an affinity with early Maya horizons, Mamón and Chicanel at Uaxactún in the Petén, contrasting with a low correlation of traits in the early ceramics of the Mexican Highlands. Middle Tres Zapotes, for Drucker, was a transitional period following local traditions rather than outside influences although characterized by new polychrome pottery. The Upper phase showed continued elaboration of polychrome types together with an influx of traits from Teotihuacan in the Mexican Plateau. It terminated before the advent of Fine Orange and Plumbate wares which came to Mesoamerica, along with metallurgy, just before A. D. 1000.

After a study of the sherd collections from La Venta, following his war service, Drucker (1947) related La Venta ceramics to Middle Tres Zapotes. This, in turn, he had already placed with the early Classic Maya Tzakol period (A. D. 300-650 in the GMT correlation). This position was thought untenable, of course, by those who held that La Venta should have an earlier, Preclassic date.

When Robert Wauchope (1950) of Tulane University assigned La Venta to the Preclassic in a synthesizing study of Preclassic ceramics, Drucker was aghast. In print (Drucker 1952), he blamed his colleague for Wauchope's alleged misunderstanding. We can imagine that Weiant's heartbeat quickened as he penned his reply:

> . . . when Drucker, despite his assertion that he does not mean to be unfair, creates the impression that just about everything I did in the field was wrong, and that my interpretations are either dubious or one-hundred per cent erroneous, I am compelled to object. [1952: 57]

The interchange, though lively, did little to clear up the fundamental question of when La Venta was active.

Stirling's Later Discoveries

The 1943 field season was the fifth for Stirling in southern Mexico and his third involving work at La Venta. This time he was assisted by archaeologist Waldo Wedel of the Smithsonian Institution. Stirling and Wedel did not seek ceramic, but architectural sequences. Working along the centerline of the site, they uncovered two large mosaic floors which they interpreted as conventionalized jaguar masks (Stirling 1943a). Wedel unraveled the puzzle of mounds and courts constantly remodeled with brightly colored clays and columnar basalt. In 1943, Stirling (1943b: 321) still held that the La Venta culture "developed side by side with that of the Old Empire Maya, but differed widely in most respects."

Stirling spent the following 1944 season exploring in the state of Tabasco the area between the Olmec and Maya zones, seeking in vain to mesh La Venta and Maya chronology (Stirling 1947). The westernmost Maya site, Comalcalco, offered nothing comparable to La Venta, nor did any other site he visited. For the first time in many years the *Geographic* carried no September article on Stirling's work of the previous summer.

However, the fates were to smile once more on Stirling. In 1945, he returned to the Pacific side of the Isthmus of Tehuantepec at Izapa where he had worked briefly in 1941. As before, he was drawn there by stone reliefs that, while not Olmec, had an Olmec look about them. At Piedra Parada, in highland Chiapas, he sought other examples of the Olmec-like style. The stones of the Pacific slope show anecdotal scenes similar to motifs found on reliefs from the Tres Zapotes, Veracruz, site. Their stylistic development appears to grow out of the Olmec genesis.

Despite their importance, these discoveries were but a prelude to what awaited Stirling on the Gulf Coast. On his return he explored the Río Chiquito region inland from the coast between Tres Zapotes and La Venta (Fig. 1). At the small new settlement of Tenochtitlan — named after the ancient Aztec capital — the village schoolmaster showed him a collection of antiquities from the surrounding area. The collection contained Olmec pieces. Moreover, an erotic Olmec monolith (Fig. 19) was displayed in the town. Although the piece was badly broken, enough thematic material remained to show what its destroyers — Precolumbian puritans, perhaps — might have wished to occult: coitus between jaguar and human. Stirling (1947: 158) described the find more delicately to readers of the *Geographic* as "a large stone figure consisting of an anthropomorphic jaguar seated on a human figure lying on its back." The euphemistic reference deprived his public of a significant insight into Olmec ideology, namely the *raison d'être* for sculptures of human infants with jaguar mouths and other feline features. Olmec mythology surely spoke of jaguar ancestors.

This was just the beginning. Close to Tenochtitlan lay a site that was to surpass La Venta in size and richness of Olmec monoliths: San Lorenzo. At San Lorenzo the townspeople of Tenochtitlan directed Stirling to that Olmec hallmark — nothing less than another Colossal Head. With this, three sites were known to contain these gigantic sculptures: Tres Zapotes, La Venta, and San Lorenzo. The Colossal Head at San Lorenzo apparently had been purposely rolled down into a ravine where it came to rest face up. Because of its nine-foot height and imposing demeanor, the people of Tenochtitlan dubbed it "El Rey" — the king.

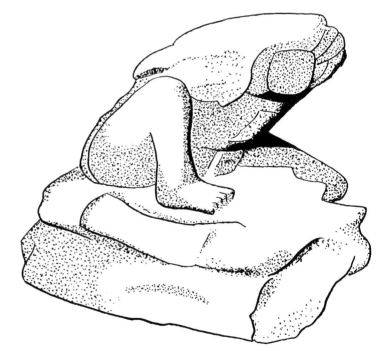

Fig. 19. Monument 1, Río Chiquito

Fig. 20. Anthropomorphic jaguar, San Lorenzo

Other sculpture quickly came to light. In all of it La Venta themes were repeated in the same pitted basalt. A tabletop altar the size of those at La Venta showed a figure seated in an arched niche and holding an infant. A second infant was held in the arms of a free figure. Other sculpture uncovered at San Lorenzo in 1945 comprised a seated anthropomorphic jaguar four feet tall (Fig. 20), a three-foot realistic head broken at the neck and wearing a flat headdress, a swimming duck with

Fig. 21. Monument 11, San Lorenzo

engraved designs, a headless figure with a cylindrical bar in its lap (Fig. 21), and a rectangular slab with carved celt-shaped depressions.

Sensing that more Olmec monoliths awaited him in the soil of San Lorenzo, Stirling came back in the 1946 season. His intuition had not failed him. The same ravine which gave up the Colossal Head of the previous season yielded *four* additional ones "better made and better preserved than any we had discovered on our previous explorations of La Venta culture" (Stirling 1947: 171).

Philip Drucker, just back from the war, accompanied Stirling in 1946. Again Drucker's aim was to collect pottery from stratigraphic trenches. Once more, as at La Venta, he was not allowed to study the ceramic material. Drucker was recalled to active service in the U.S. Navy. He was to administer a Pacific Island.

Except that the pottery remained unstudied, the 1946 season was fruitful. The enormity of San Lorenzo was revealed as Stirling and Drucker cleared and mapped its principal mounds and plazas. Nearby they discovered another important Olmec site, Potrero Nuevo. Here the erotic theme of Tenochtitlan was repeated in a second wrecked statue of a copulating jaguar and human (Fig. 22). A tabletop altar revealed two chubby dwarfs holding up the overhanging ledge with raised hands (Fig. 23). An elongated sitting jaguar and a seated human holding a serpent completed the monuments.

This was to be Stirling's last trip into Olmec country. Plaster casts of the Colossal Heads were placed in the National Geographic Society headquarters in Washington to flank "Explorers' Hall." They pay fitting tribute to the man who carried the tradition of the explorers of Mexico in the 1800s — Stephens, Seler, Charney, Holmes — into a century characterized by archaeological specialization and in which exploring is no longer quite fashionable.

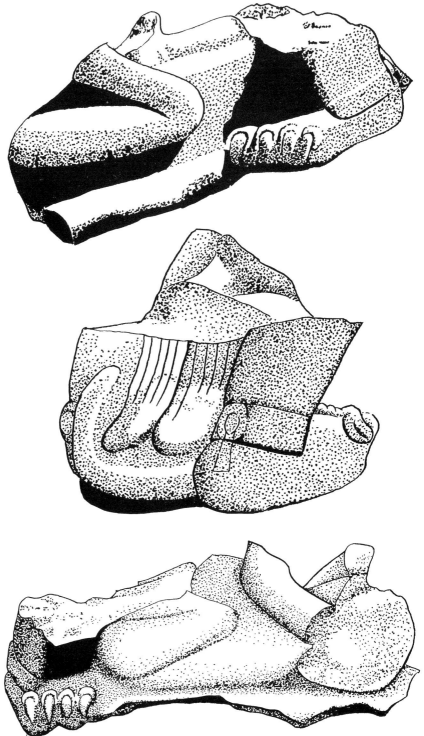

Fig. 22. Monument 3, Potrero Nuevo

Fig. 23. Dwarf altar, Potrero Nuevo

Nuclear Physics and Tlatilco

Events outside the La Venta area were now to shape opinions about the Olmec. In the immediate postwar years at the University of Chicago, Libby and Arnold perfected a technique for measuring minute radiations. By 1948 the method had been adapted to determine, through measurement of radiocarbon content, the age of organic specimens recovered archaeologically. Carbon samples proved that in the Valley of Mexico agriculturists of Preclassic culture were settled in villages at least by 1500 B.C. — much earlier than anyone had thought possible.

A second relevant happening of the years during Stirling's explorations was the discovery of an extensive early cemetery just outside Mexico City. Brickmakers had stumbled across it, and immediately built up a flourishing business in antiquities. One of their customers was Miguel Covarrubias. He regularly visited the Tlatilco brickyard vying with collectors such as Fred Fields, Kurt Stavenhagen, George Pepper, and Diego Rivera for purchase of charming pottery figurines and graceful vessels. Although many of the artifacts were Preclassic like those known from Vaillant's excavations in the 1930s at nearby sites Zacatenco and El Arbolillo, Covarrubias (1943) noted that others were of Olmec style.

Because of Tlatilco's obvious importance in illuminating the Olmec problem, Covarrubias urged scientific excavations. Not until 1947 was he able to rally support for an adequate program. With Mexican archaeologist Rubín de la Borbolla, Covarrubias by January, 1950, had directed the unearthing of 203 graves. The excavations showed the presence of an elite in the Valley of Mexico during Middle Preclassic times. Within archaeological contexts the humble wares of the El Arbolillo and Zacatenco peasants lay in the same strata as the sophisticated wares of the rich grave offerings in the Tlatilco cemetery.

The elite culture showed no development within the Valley, but rather a sudden introduction from outside. Specific traits pointed to the Gulf Coast as a possible source and to the bearers of Olmec culture as the elite themselves. Tlatilco graves shared many features with La Venta. Among these were: rare "rocker-stamped" pottery, tiger masks, figures of dwarfs, figures with "football helmets," Vaillant's type A figurines (Porter 1953: 31), use of cinnabar, miniature hematite mirrors on figurines, representations of adults holding infants (Drucker, Heizer and Squire 1959: 258), and bearded figures (Piña 1955: Fig. 6).

But the findings at Tlatilco could be interpreted in several ways. One archaeologist who had worked at Tlatilco, Muriel

Porter (1953: 52), followed Drucker in saying Olmec influence there "must have come from a Pre-Classic Olmec culture which already possessed many features to be manifested later at La Venta." Drucker, himself, wrote his La Venta report while the Tlatilco explorations were in progress. He had seen only part of the Tlatilco artifacts (Drucker, Heizer and Squire 1959: 255) and while continuing to favor a La Venta-Tzakol (Early Maya Classic) correlation, he was bothered by doubt (1952: 255), "The Tlatilco-Olmec material which stylistically is surely referable to the La Venta-Middle Tres Zapotes horizon hints that one side or the other of our time scale is wrong."

Covarrubias and other proponents of a Preclassic situation of La Venta held that the Tlatilco investigations confirmed their view. La Venta needed to be looked at in a new light, one made more brilliant by the radiocarbon technique.

The Far-flung Olmec Presence

The extent of the Olmec style was only beginning to be recognized. J. Eric Thompson (1943: 111) had published a relief from San Isidro Piedra Parada (Fig. 24) near Quetzaltenango, Guatemala, similar in pose, dress, and facial features to the marginal figures on Stela 2 from La Venta, Tabasco (Fig. 7). Stanley Boggs (1950), prompted by Stirling's La Venta reliefs, reported others of Olmec style found from even farther south at Las Victorias near Chalchuapa, El Salvador. Over 200 miles from La Venta to the north another Olmec relief (Fig. 13) would be turned up in 1960 by masons laying a tile floor in a patio at El Viejón, Actopan, Veracruz (Medellín 1960: 80-81, Pl. 9). These finds, taken with Waterman's stela from El Baul, Guatemala, indicate a north-south extension of Olmec influence of 600 miles.

Related to the problem of how far Olmec style reaches is that of finding the boundaries of the Olmec heartland, the area showing sites of the La Venta pattern. Ranging to the southeast

Fig. 24. Drawing and rubbings
by Roberto Ibarra of relief carving
from Chalchuapa, El Salvador

across the state of Tabasco in 1944, Stirling had found no Olmec sites. A more intensive search was needed to determine the eastern and southern boundaries of the heartland; and so Philip Drucker and Mexican archaeologist Eduardo Contreras set out in the dry season of 1953. In 100 days they rode 700 miles by mule and located ninety sites. Starting on the east at Huimanguillo on the Grijalva River, they followed the major streams lying between the Grijalva and the Coatzacoalcos. Drucker and Contreras's (1953: 396) impression was that the savannah country inland from the coast had prevented the expansion of the Olmec heartland so that it was restricted to the coastal strip between Laguna del Carmen and the Papaloapan River (Fig. 1).

More Work at La Venta

Not until 1955 did a new attack on La Venta get under way. Heading it were Drucker and Robert Heizer, an archaeologist with many years of field experience in California. Excavation of the shell middens along California's coast requires close attention to subtle changes in stratigraphy. Archaeological techniques as practiced in California were ideally suited to La Venta where, at variance with most of Mesoamerica, the architecture has no stone veneer. Subtle changes in the soils forming the platform mounds of La Venta held the key to understanding construction sequences.

Mound profiles could be exposed only with the expenditure of much human labor over a long time. In the largest and most enduring operation ever carried out at La Venta, Drucker and Heizer worked from mid-January to late May 1955, using fifty laborers for 100 working days (Drucker, Heizer, and Squire 1959: 2). In addition, a bulldozer lent by Petróleos Mexicanos shoved aside some of the three-foot, gray sand overburden on the Central Court.

An excavated monolith, Monument 19, bore a masterfully executed design which, as in many La Venta reliefs, follows in its composition the form of the original block. A giant stylized serpent, with rattlers that would have sounded like thunderclaps, held protectively an Olmec personage within the arc of its body (Fig. 25).

A cache of smaller stone sculptures indicated how Olmec figurines might have functioned. A group of sixteen male figurines arranged in front of six celts, Offering No. 4, surely represented a ritual.

The work of the 1955 season provided the first accurate description of La Venta. The picture which emerged shows as the largest feature at the site a pyramid 420 by 240 feet and over 100 feet high (Fig. 17). To the north lies a plaza flanked by two long low mounds running north-south for about 300 feet. Farther along, parallel rows of basalt columns 185 feet apart run another 135 feet. Closing the northern end of the "Ceremonial Court" formed by the columnar wall is a large mound (A-2) in which Stirling found a tomb of basalt columns and a sarcophagus bearing an Olmec mask relief (Fig. 15). Both mortuary features in the middle of the courts are aligned 8 degrees west of north like the rest of the site. The 1955 excavators focused along this center axis.

Drucker and Heizer dug enormous trenches down through structures to the native soil. Profiles disclosed how the platforms and pyramids were built up of successive constructions. The bulk of the final report consists of text describing detailed foldout drawings of such profiles.

It was the same sort of careful excavation that cleared up the mystery of the tiger masks. In 1943 Stirling and Wedel had uncovered two mosaic stone pavements in the form of tiger masks, but had failed to understand their significance. One of these lay buried along the centerline just north of the principal pyramid; another beneath a small mound east of the centerline. Because the site generally displays a bilaterally symmetrical ground plan, Drucker and Heizer were convinced that a

Fig. 25. Monument 19, La Venta

third mosaic floor rested beneath a mound west of centerline in a position corresponding to the eastern one.

Having been told what they were digging for, the workmen were dumbfounded when, exactly as predicted, their picks and shovels revealed a third tiger mask. They were convinced that surveying instruments provided the archaeologists with X-ray vision.

More fascinating than the mask itself was its context. The small mound had sat upon a pit 62 feet square and 26 feet deep. In addition to the mask, the pit was filled with layers of colored clay, adobe bricks and 28 layers of green serpentine slabs, the latter weighing an estimated 1200 tons (Heizer 1961: 44). Apparently this "massive offering" was laid down all at once. Moreover, the tons of stone would have had to be carried into the alluvial zone; the closest green serpentine deposits yet found are on the Pacific side of the Isthmus of Tehuantepec.

Four building phases were determined for La Venta from the study of trench profiles. Only after this sequence had emerged were charcoal samples collected for radiocarbon dating thereby allowing a known context for each. For the first time the epoch of the building of La Venta was revealed.

Drucker and Heizer (1956: 367) guessed that the earliest date would fall around the time of Christ, and the latest five centuries later. Such dates were generally in accord with the idea that La Venta flourished during the Maya Early Classic. As things turned out, the archaeologists' chronological reckonings hit wide of the mark; the radiocarbon analysis indicated that they fell almost a millennium too late!

Nine radiocarbon dates pointed to La Venta's construction during a span from 800 to 400 B.C. Covarrubias and Caso had been correct. In their final report (Drucker, Heizer, and Squire 1959: 260-61) the excavators were forced to admit, "The C-14 dates presented here indicate that Drucker's estimate of the chronological position of the La Venta horizon was wrong; the Mayan specialists who placed it even later were likewise in error."

With this Drucker retired from archaeology, isolating himself from the world as much as is possible in the present day, to raise cattle some fifteen hours upriver by launch from Coatzacoalcos.

Laguna de los Cerros

Midway between the Olmec sites of Tres Zapotes and San Lorenzo, Mexican archaeologist Alfonso Medellín Zenil discovered another Olmec center: Laguna de los Cerros. Financed by the University of Veracruz, Medellín (1960) worked at the site from March 13 to May 8, 1960. He unearthed twenty-seven monoliths and mapped ninety-five mounds revealing Laguna de los Cerros as a center that may have rivaled La Venta and San Lorenzo. An altar of the same form as those found at the latter sites appeared along the central axis of Laguna de los Cerros. Its characteristic projecting top and figure seated within a niche relate it to the other Olmec tabletop altars (Fig. 26). A free-standing, larger-than-life image wears a breechclout and the cape that typifies personages on Olmec reliefs. Two seated figures also appear to be within the Olmec tradition (Fig. 27).

Despite their undeniable Olmec stylistic affinity, Medellín holds that since some of these monuments were in association with Upper Tres Zapotes ceramics, they must be placed in late Classic times. If, indeed, the ceramic association is correct, a more plausible explanation would be that the monuments were removed from an Olmec context in late Classic times.

Later Discoveries

Sometime after the beginning of 1965, rumors reached Jalapa, the capital of Veracruz, that another Colossal Head had been found in San Lorenzo. Medellín was dispatched by the State Museum of Jalapa to investigate. Accompanied by archaeologist Román Piña Chan of the National Institute of

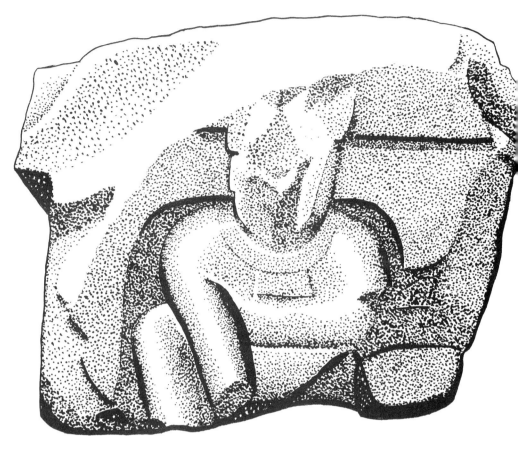

Fig. 26. Monolith 5, Laguna de los Cerros

Anthropology and History, Medellín made the long journey upriver from Coatzacoalcos. The trip was not made in vain. Halfway up the slope of a ravine, on the western edge of the site, rested face down the sixth Colossal Head to be found at San Lorenzo. Clearly within the local tradition it showed the same serene expression, cipher-like ears, and wide-banded helmet of the other San Lorenzo Heads (Medellín 1965).

Later in the year, on July 16, 1965, two children made an important discovery south of San Lorenzo at Las Limas, Veracruz. Las Limas rests beside a tributary of the Coatzacoalcos,

Fig. 27. Monolith 8, Laguna de los Cerros

the Río Jaltepec, near the town of Jesús Carranza. Many of the huts of the village are built upon ancient mounds which offer protection from the damp soil. Atop one of the mounds, Rosa Salazar and her little brother Severiano cracked *coyol* husks on a round green stone that poked out of the ground. Deciding that they would take the rock home with them, the two scooped up the earth around it. Suddenly a face of stone stared at them. They had discovered one of the masterpieces of Olmec art: a male figure over a half-meter high, holding an infant on its crossed legs (Fig. 28). Authorities from the Jalapa Museum encountered the statue set within an elaborate altar in the Salazar hut. A silken cape graced its shoulders and paper flowers and burning candles were set before it. Now in the Museum, the monument clearly relates to the Olmec tabletop altars that show infants in arms, as well as to smaller sculptures in New York's Museum of Primitive Art and in the Brooklyn Museum (Beltrán 1965).

Carefully planned excavations at San Lorenzo were initiated in 1966. With financial support from the National Science Foundation, Michael Coe of Yale University began the first of three seasons of work at the three sites along the Río Chiquito: Tenochtitlan, San Lorenzo, and Potrero Nuevo. Engineer Raymond Krotser began the accurate mapping of the sites while field director Richard Diehl and archaeologists Francisco Beverido and Paula Krotser located and dug stone monuments.

Their digging differed from that of Stirling and Drucker two decades earlier. At San Lorenzo painstaking work revealed the all-important contexts of monuments. For example, Monument 21, a rectangular block with hollow back, was shown to have been deliberately placed at the head of a ravine. Beneath it lay an offering of seven serpentine celts, pottery vessels, and charcoal. The picture that emerged was not that of a frantic destruction of the site as previously supposed, but rather a peaceful and purposeful ritualistic interment of the sculptures

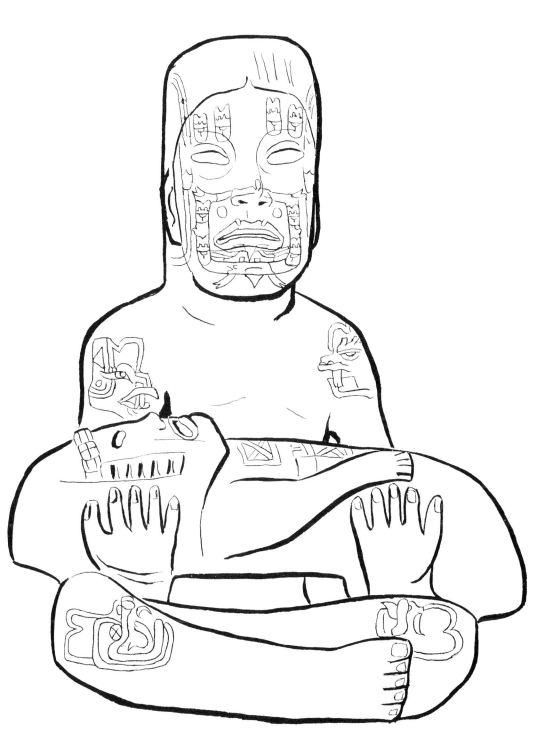

Fig. 28. Babe in Arms, stone figurine

(Coe 1966). Furthermore, the carbon underlying the monuments enabled their deposition there to be dated through radiocarbon analysis. Corroborative evidence in the form of pottery sherds was collected and recorded as well.

What did charcoal and ceramics show? After a study of the sherds at the National Museum in Mexico City during June and July, Coe concluded that they are very much like those from the Cuadros and Jocotal phases of Pacific Coast Guatemala dated by radiocarbon between 1000 and 800 B.C. The San Lorenzo radiocarbon dates, which were forthcoming later, supported the preliminary conclusion. Of six samples, five fell between 1200 and 850 B.C. (Coe, personal communication). Relative to the radiocarbon dates from La Venta of 800 to 400 B.C., the Olmec occupation of San Lorenzo seems directly to precede that at La Venta.

Completely unexpected was the find of a retired steel executive, Carlo Gay, and Gillett Griffin, curator of graphic arts at Princeton University. In a Guerrero cave the two hit upon Olmec mural paintings. Up until the 1966 discovery, the earliest known Mesoamerican murals from the Maya zone and Teotihuacan dated several centuries after Christ. Now, Gay and Griffin's revelation pushed back the date to several centuries before Christ.

Since his retirement in 1961, Gay had dedicated himself to the study of the Olmec; he reported on new findings of reliefs at Chalcatzingo, Morelos (Gay 1966). In 1963, tracing rumors of cave paintings, he was led to Colotlipa, Guerrero, seventy-five miles northeast of the Pacific resort Acapulco. There he and Griffin met one Andrés Ortega, self-appointed curator of the murals. Ortega guided the pair to the Juxtlahuaca Cave.

Together, they entered chamber after dark chamber filled with nothing more than roaches and the squeak and flutter, and the dung, of myriad bats. After a kilometer of sinuous groping, their lamps revealed the earliest painting in the New World (Gay 1967): a large polychrome of two human figures.

Farther within the cave, a red crouching feline and a red snake with green feathered brow were reflected in the lamplight. In all, three paintings and three line drawings were discovered. One of the drawings, a charcoal outline, looks as if it were abandoned before painting by a Renaissance master. Nude save for a breechclout, with feet astride and the right hand holding aloft an enigmatic object, the masculine figure is stylistically Olmec. Its flowing lines, narrow sloping shoulders, ample hips, and jutting neck all stamp it as such.

For the jaguar and serpent the stylistic identification is not as certain because of the lack of comparative materials. Certainly their context argues well for their being Olmec.

What meaning lies behind these images? The snake and jaguar, apparently squaring off at one another, could represent one of the many dualities in Mesoamerican religion. In Aztec thought the jaguar symbolized the night and the red serpent the dawn or Venus as the morning star. Perhaps the Juxlahuaca Cave paintings reveal the antiquity of the Mesoamerican religious concept of antagonistic forces.

The significance of the composition of standing and kneeling figures seems more tenuous (Fig. 29). The erect personage — over five feet tall — wears a quetzal-plumed, chin-strapped, helmet from which protrude disc earplugs. A dark cape over one shoulder half covers a shift of broad horizontal stripes alternating in red, ocher, and neutral. What might be jaguar skin covers the limbs, and forms the breechclout hanging from beneath the shift. Dress and pose are rather like that of the Olmec reliefs at Chalchuapa, El Salvador (Fig. 24). From the left hand a rope crosses the body.

The cord is attached to the wide belt of the smaller individual sitting with crossed legs. His physical type contrasts with that of the larger figure in his aquiline nose and goatee. It is the same seen on Stela 3, La Venta (Fig. 9); and the nude figure on the Chalcatzingo reliefs (Fig. 11). His black face in later times would mean that he is a priest or a warrior. The rope and his

Fig. 29. Mural painting, Juxtlahuaca Cave

inferior position relative to the standing personage point to his being a captive. The theme on Altar 4 at La Venta (Fig. 8) is repeated; that of seventh-century Maya murals at Bonampak is prefigured.

Yet, why is such a scene depicted deep within a cavern? Did the same mechanism of sympathetic magic that guaranteed success in the hunt to Paleolithic painters of Altamira and Lascaux promise victory to Olmec soldiers? Or do the paintings mark a rite of passage for a young warrior on the capture of his first prisoner? If so, the rite would have taken place within Juxtlahuaca Cave a millennium and a half before Gay and Griffin entered there.

More on the Olmec Problem

What are the ultimate origins of the Olmec development? Coe's work locates the beginnings of Olmec culture in the heartland toward the end of the Lower Preclassic or Early Formative at San Lorenzo. Adding Coe's evidence to the radiocarbon dates from La Venta, the question of contemporaniety of Olmec and Classic Period Maya culture is no longer valid. This problem solved, however, another takes its place: Where are we to look for the antecedents of the Olmec style? The monuments of San Lorenzo show a sophistication that suggests long development. Yet nothing leading up to them has been found in the Gulf Coast area. Given the relatively thorough archaeological investigations that we have described for the region, this is remarkable. I believe, therefore, that the origins must be sought elsewhere.

But where is one to look? Gordon Ekholm (1964: 503-4), curator of Mexican archaeology at the American Museum of Natural History, suggests early bronze-age China as a "likely prospect." In the art of the Shang dynasty (sixteenth century B.C. to 1027 B.C.) the feline motif is prominent. Delight in highly polished jade objects was also shared by the Shang and Olmec peoples.

More is known of Shang dynasty culture than that of its Mexican contemporaries. Perhaps this is one reason why Ekholm and his colleague Heine-Geldern were attracted to early China as a possible source for Olmec style.

Most Americanists adopt a more conservative posture and look within Mesoamerica for the origins of Olmec culture. At present, three distinct Mesoamerican subareas suggest themselves. Caso (1964: 13) and Coe (1965: 122) argue for the Olmec heartland of southern Veracruz and northern Tabasco. Caso sees the region as a geographically favored one akin to the Nile Valley, the Tigris-Euphrates floodplain, and the Indus and Hwang-Ho Valleys of the Old World which gave birth to urban civilization. Coe opts for the Gulf Coast region because it is here that the great florescence of Olmec art takes place.

A second possibility is championed by Román Piña Chan (1955: 106). After hypothesizing complex movements of peoples to account for the archaeological distribution of Olmec remains, Piña concludes that the Olmec originated in central Mexico within or near the state of Morelos.

A third view, that of Covarrubias (1957: 76), holds that the Pacific slopes of Oaxaca and Guerrero spawned the Olmec style "where its most archaic forms appear." In attacking the position, Coe (1965b: 122) asserts that Covarrubias's view "was based on the wholly unwarranted assumption that small-scale always precedes large-scale art." Actually Covarrubias speaks of style, not size.

None of the theses, however, seems free of objections. Against Caso's position we may note that the geographical conditions in which Old World civilizations were nurtured are not duplicated in the Olmec heartland; the rivers are present, but not the deserts. Opposing Coe's claim is the unlikely presence of examples of monumental art arising far from their ultimate source as do the giant heads of Easter Island. Clouding both Piña Chan's and Covarrubias' arguments is the distressing fact that the areas they favor are virtually unknown archaeologically. Certainly a study of the evolution of Olmec style is intimately related to the problem of origins. To anticipate, our findings bear out Covarrubias, although pointing more toward Oaxaca than to Guerrero.

Our evolutionary scheme not only should contribute to the clarification of the beginnings of Olmec style, but to its demise as well. Medellín's situating Laguna de los Cerros sculpture in the Classic Period dramatizes the lack of agreement as to when Olmec culture ended.

Without carrying the Olmec style into the Classic, other authorities nonetheless vary widely in their estimates for the termination of Olmec culture. Basing his views on the radio-carbon dates from La Venta, Heizer (1961: 54) sees 400 B.C. as a likely date. Wigberto Jiménez Moreno (1957: 1031) chooses 200 B.C. after considering in detail the comparative archaeology of the Mexican lowlands. Art historian George Kubler (1962a: xxxiii) places the end of the Olmec style at A.D. 300 because of its influence on that of the early Maya.*
Two U.S. archaeologists, Proskouriakoff (1963) and Lathrop (1964) summarily dismiss Kubler's thesis on the grounds that it ignores archaeological data.

Even more difficult to elucidate than chronology is the question of the kind of society that created the Olmec style. We know that Mesoamerica — a culture area embracing central and southern Mexico and adjoining parts of Central America as far as Costa Rica — was characterized by early civilization, but just how early? This society, with social stratification, speci-alists, writing, cities, and great art styles, is clearly visible in the archaeological record of the Mesoamerican Classic Period in the first millennium after Christ. In the millennium before

---

*The Spinden correlation for Maya dates is thought by some to coincide more with the view of an Olmec-Maya overlap than the more widely accepted Goodman-Martínez-Thompson correlation, because it sets the beginning of the Maya Classic 260 years earlier. Nevertheless, it would also push back 260 years the dated Olmec monuments such as Stela C from Tres Zapotes.

Christ, when San Lorenzo and La Venta flourished, the record is relatively unclear.

Was there an Olmec civilization? Two schools have formed around this question. One, for which Coe speaks, sees the beginning of a non-urban Mesoamerican civilization with the Olmecs in the tropical lowlands. The other, championed by William Sanders (1963: 973), holds that ecological conditions in the tropics would not allow civilizations to emerge, arguing that it is only in the highlands with the discovery of irrigation that sufficient conditions were present to permit urbanization from which could follow a non-urban lowland development of civilization.

If art reflects the society that produces it, an analysis of Olmec art should provide insights into the character of Olmec society. Before attempting this, however, it is necessary to examine the basic premises about art and style that underlie such considerations.

2

Art and Style

"ART" HAS MANY MEANINGS and covers many of man's creations. For the Olmec this range has been narrowed by the ravages of time. Olmec music and literature are forever lost to us. Only the visual plastic arts can be treated in a study of Olmec art because they are the only ones that have survived.

But just how are we to go about such a study? One pitfall in the anthropological approach — although quite a legitimate procedure in others — is that of making aesthetic judgments. In looking at Olmec sculpture we do not search for beauty, although it may be there. To qualify as art, a product need not be beautiful. Witness the work of Mexican muralists Orozco and Siqueiros; it shows power and rage, but beauty?

One's idea of beauty is a product of his culture. Oriental canons differ from Western ones; Polynesian from African. This is reason enough to set aside Western values when treating an exotic style that developed in isolation from Old World traditions.

Having discarded the concept of beauty, what criteria are left to us with which to characterize art? Actually many definitions of art do not incorporate the idea of beauty. Munro (1949: 59), in a detailed analysis of definitions, lists one of these as being "the broad aesthetic non-evaluative meaning of 'art'." This is "the practice of any of the fine or aesthetic arts, or the product of such practices." Surely Olmec stone carvings resulted from the practice of the fine art of sculpture. No one would argue against this, so self-evident does it seem. Munro's non-evaluative meaning indeed appears to be so dispassionate as to have almost no significance.

It is included here because it does lead to the question of why, as in the case of Olmec sculpture, does one know that this is the product of the practice of one of the fine or aesthetic arts? Such knowledge is not instinctive, it is based on observation. What is observed is that a standard of technical excellence has been achieved that has allowed typical or fixed forms to be created (Boas 1955: 10).

Panofsky (1955: 10) has pointed out that: "A work of art is not always created exclusively for the purpose of being enjoyed . . . but . . . always *has* aesthetic significance (not to be confused with aesthetic value): whether or not it serves some practical purpose, and whether it is good or bad, it demands to be experienced aesthetically." According to Panofsky, all man-made objects have an "intention," and they may be either practical or works of art. Both practical objects and works of art may be further divided into "vehicles of communication, and tools or apparatuses" (p. 12). Among works of art, for example, "a poem or an historical painting is, in a sense, a vehicle of communication; the Pantheon and the Milan candlesticks are, in a sense, apparatuses" (p. 12). Olmec sculpture, as we shall see, is, in a sense, not only art but a vehicle of communication as well.

Obviously, the investigator encounters many borderline cases: aesthetically pleasing tools, for example, which show technical excellence and fixity of form. What was the primary intention of the toolmaker? Panofsky (p. 13) admits that the intention of the creators of artifacts, which determines whether their products are primarily practical objects or art, cannot be arrived at absolutely.

In the first place, "intentions" are, *per se*, incapable of being defined with scientific precision. In the second place, the "intentions" of those who produce objects are conditioned by the standards of their period and environment . . . . Finally our estimate of those "intentions" is inevitably influenced by our own attitude, which in turn depends on our individual experiences as well as on our historical situation.

Art and Anthropology

It is precisely in the domain of "the standards of their period and environment" and "our individual experiences as well as . . . historical tradition" that the anthropologist can best make a contribution to studies of art history, for this is the realm of culture. Culture to the anthropologist means "shared patterns of learned behavior" (Gorer in Kroeber and Kluckhohn 1961: 108). This learned, shared behavior is "manifest in act and artifact" (Redfield in Kroeber and Kluckhohn 1961: 118). Such acts and artifacts, because they result from learning and sharing, are not capricious, but are instead part of cultural tradition. "Cultural tradition [is] the process by which in a given socal group or social class language, beliefs, ideas, aesthetic tastes, knowledge, skills and usages of many kinds are handed on ('tradition' means 'handing on') from person to person and from one generation to another" (Radcliffe-Brown in Kroeber and Kluckhohn 1961: 92).

Art is a part of this cultural tradition. The meanings of its symbols and themes are learned and shared, just as language is learned and shared. A person who babbles in an unknown tongue cannot function in a society; an artist who completely abandons traditional symbols can have no large public, no honest patrons, and no significant work in a society because, like the babbler, he cannot be understood. Whereas all culture change, including innovation in language and in art, takes place at the locus of interaction between individuals, no one individual seems capable of reshaping his culture more than slightly.

This is the reason that art presents a history that can be studied. It is the reason that a style changes or evolves gradually and so may be traced through time. The history of art is the history of styles.

It is a commonplace that art production often is irrational or nonrational. If this be so, art nevertheless remains within the provenience of culture because culture embraces the nonrational. The idea that culture includes more than rational behavior marks a relatively recent advance in culture theory. Kluckhohn and Kelly (in Kroeber and Kluckhohn 1961: 97) express it emphatically: "By culture we mean all those historically created designs for living, explicit and implicit, rational, irrational, and nonrational, which exist at any given time as potential guides for the behavior of men."

But the views of anthropologists are not necessarily shared by other specialists. George Kubler probably echoes the sentiments of his fellow art historians when he objects to anthropologists' relegation of art to a mere aspect of culture. He speaks of one anthropologist's view of culture as a "deity working his wonders to perform" with the implication that "art is mere illustration, and the art object is *determined* by its cultural context." He continues (comment on Haselberger 1961: 370):

It remains the view of many art historians, however, that no theory of historical change can be valid if it fails to account for those indeterminate or mutational aspects of happening of which important works of art have always been our clearest evidence. [We] suggest the absolute primacy of artistic activity as an exploratory mode of sensing the universe. This mode may be shaped by culture, to be sure, but it exists independently and outside many of the stock responses of cultural conditioning. In contrast to the anthropologist, who shelves art under culture, the art historian always wants to invert this order, by looking to artists for the clearest manifestations of those non-rational impulses toward change without which there can be no history. Art [transcends] its cultural framework whenever it is a prime object rather than a replica of another object.

I hold that most art production involves replication. Where change does take place in art, it is rarely if ever *totus in toto*, but for the most part involves regrouping of elements or slight additions to, and subtractions from them. Indeed, anthropological theory dealing with culture change is largely concerned with recombinations of already existing elements to bring about innovations.

Kubler appears to have shifted toward the tenets of anthropological theory of culture change when writing a year later on the subject of new evidence in the field of linguistics that languages change regularly and at a constant velocity. This linguistic "drift" is explained by cybernetic theory as being "produced by cumulative change in the articulation of sounds [and] can be related in turn to the interferences that destroy any audible communication" (Kubler 1962b: 60). In summary (p. 61):

These recent developments in the historical theory of language require us to reconsider the position of works of art as historical evidence. Most kinds of historical happenings are subject to incalculable interferences which deprive history of the scope of predictive science. Linguistic structures, however, admit only those interferences whose regularity will not interfere with communication. The history of things, in turn, admits more interferences than language, but fewer than institutional history, because things which must serve functions and convey messages cannot be diverted from these finalities without loss of identity.

Within the history of things we find the history of art. More than tools, works of art resemble a system of symbolic communication which must be free from excessive "noise" in the many copies upon which communication depends, in order to ensure some fidelity. Because of its intermediate position between general history and linguistic science, the history of art may eventually prove to contain unexpected potentialities as a predictable science, less productive than linguistics, but more so than can ever be possible in general history.

In the present consideration of Olmec art, I seek to show that changes in art are similar to changes in any realm of culture, that they are regular and constant, not haphazard and capricious. I concur with Kubler's view that art is a form of symbolic communication and that, in this, it is closely akin to language.

Linguistic studies have received much attention from anthropologists. Quantities of data have been collected, yet no direct relationship of linguistic structure to other aspects of culture such as social structure has been demonstrated. Perhaps no such relationship exists. At any rate, the same problem in the field of art is probably much further from solution. At present, no evidence points to a direct relationship between art style and socio-political structure.

The evolution of art styles seems to be of the same nature as changes in language about which relatively more is known. This similarity holds because an artist cannot divorce himself from society. He must produce for a public. The themes he chooses must be conditioned by his clientele. This holds even today in complex societies. Socialist realism is produced in the Soviet Union because the ruling hierarchy demands propagandistic art. Expressionist and other non-representational movements of the West flourish because some patrons value novelty *per se*, and view anything "new" as "good." The individualism of recent Western art movements, although actually not as particular as it appears to the superficial observer, often seems to reflect a reaction against regimentation, discipline, standardization, mass production, and industrial precision. Yet in reacting, this individualism is conditioned by society.

True, circumstances prevail today that have unique consequences for art production. For the first time in human history examples of almost all surviving art styles are available to artists through museums and publications. Mass production technology combined with far-reaching distributive networks makes art available to a giant public in periodicals, motion pictures, phonograph records, and books. Differences in taste characterize different social classes, age groups, occupation and other interest groups so that, as never before, many publics are available to the artist. Today in the U.S., for example, such diverse graphic styles are accommodated as those of Walt Disney, Norman Rockwell, Pablo Picasso, and Jackson Pollock.

The parallels of art and language extend over into this heterogenous complexity; diverse "styles" of speaking have resulted from the isolation of certain social groups. Not only do scientists employ special vocabularies and manners of speaking among themselves; so do the military, advertising men, homosexuals, actors, and criminals. Writers have individual styles, but the literary style of an epoch, such as that of the Victorian novel, can be characterized in general. Art and language are alike in possessing style.

Style

Depending on its context, *style* can take on one of two general meanings: that of an absolute or that of a variable. For our purposes we need not formulate an absolute definition. Apart from *style* in its generic sense, the meaning of *a style* is essential to our ends. *A style* is a group of forms coherent to the beholder. The Olmec style, for example, is such a group of forms, obviously marked by a particular style.

Admittedly, the view of the beholder must be, in certain degree, subjective. It is conditioned by learning within a particular cultural context. A Rembrandt portrait with deep shadows might seem jarring to someone accustomed only to Japanese works of flat color areas. Furthermore, clinical psychologists tell us that one's psychological state conditions his perception, e.g., a psychotic will explain marginal minutiae in an ink-blot test. Despite such limitations, art styles have been studied cross-culturally by critics who although perhaps at times somewhat neurotic are less often psychotic.

What the beholder discerns when confronted by a style is a *gestalt* or configuration: an interplay of elements, a harmonious system of relationships. He observes qualities rather than quantities.

Quantification, as opposed to qualification, seems of little value in the analysis of style. Perhaps as a result of popular education, we think that tagging something with a number is the essence of scientific behavior, that somehow quantities are more real than qualities. For example, in a mania for physical and psychological measurements we ignore that these give us an inadequate picture of the individual. Nevertheless, we do not quantify friends much beyond age, weight, and earning capacity. We can feel their "true" or essential nature, even though this is difficult to put in numbers. Thus we qualify our friends more than we quantify them. In doing so, we also perceive them as wholes.

Like the individual person, a work of art is felt as a configuration, as a *gestalt*. In judging art, as in judging people, we qualify rather than quantify. Works of art are so perceived because they are not haphazard, but organized into configurations.

The elements of the configuration are affected by the manner of their inclusion, that is by their interaction with other elements. For example, a color in a painting is dark or light, bright or dull, depending on its relationship to the other colors in the painting. Art is art only because organization takes place within it. E. M. Forster (1949) has contrasted the order which is possible in art with the disorder which characterizes mankind's history and personal life. This (p. 33) is

the order which an artist can create in his own work . . . . A work of art, we are all agreed, is a unique product. But why? It is unique not because it is clever or noble or beautiful or enlightened or original or sincere or idealistic or useful or educational — it may embody any of those qualities — but because it is the only material object in the universe which may possess internal harmony . . . . It is the one orderly product which our muddling race has produced.

The artist "creates through his sensitiveness and his power to impose form . . . . [Form] alters from generation to generation. Artists always seek a new technique, and will continue to do so as long as their work excites them. But form of some kind is imperative. It is the surface crust of the internal harmony, it is the outward evidence of order" (p. 34).

The goal of perceiving configuration or *gestalt* has been important to the development of science in general. For example, Köhler (1963) notes that "such eminent physicists as C. Maxwell, M. Plank, and A. Eddington have sometimes clearly stated that a purely analytical approach may not be able to do justice to all phases of physical nature. Actually, whole sets of physical processes are treated in what could not properly be called an analytical fashion . . . ."

A Scientific Approach to Olmec Style

A style can only be defined by the appearance of its *gestalt*. At the same time, something about a particular style may be learned from analytical treatment. This course is not at cross-purposes with the configurational approach; both methodologies aim at insights into the nature of a style and the results of each should bear out the other.

For analytical purposes I intend to extract the formal components of the Olmec style. All the while, we should try to keep in mind the original relationships; otherwise the pursuit has no meaning because we lose the essence of style.

In the analysis of style, several levels may be involved, each with its separate components. A. L. Kroeber (1957: 30) sees three ingredients or levels of style:

First is the gross or objective subject matter dealt with . . . . Second is the "concept" of the subject, along with its emotional aura and its value toning. This is the factor that differentiates one portrait of a person from another painter's portrait of him . . . . This is still, in one sense content, subject matter, but it is subjective content, as felt by the artist; and in another sense it is form, the product achieved by the artist and the style . . . . And third is the specific, technical form given the work of art by the artist in his execution of it — his diction, rhythm, or brush stroke. With this ingredient we have fully entered into the realm of creativity, of aesthetic achievement.

How can these three ingredients be applied to a breakdown of Olmec style? Let us consider each of the three levels under a separate heading.

Objective Subject Matter.

Much of the subject matter in Olmec art foreshadows that of the Classic Mesoamerican styles, especially the Maya. Because of this correspondence, Olmec themes, while important, are not sufficient in themselves for a characterization of the style. Before being placed stylistically they must be perceived in the context of Kroeber's other aspects. Keeping this in mind, let us look at these Olmec themes.

Realistic humans, stylized jaguars, plus infinitely varied combinations of the two make up the bulk of Olmec objective subject matter. For Covarrubias (1957: 56) the humans conform to a "curious aesthetic ideal." He characterizes them as

plump men (very seldom women) with elongated, pear shaped heads artificially deformed and completely shaved, sometimes wearing headbands or a helmet with chin strap. The heads have short noses with perforated septums, fleshy necks, heavy jowls, and prominent, stubborn chins. Their eyes are decidedly Mongoloid, almond-shaped or narrow slits between puffed eyelids. But their most characteristic feature is a large trapezoid mouth, known among archaeologists as the "Olmec" or "jaguar" mouth, with the corners drawn downward and a thick, flaring upper lip that gives them a despondent, fierce expression like that of a snarling jaguar . . . These artists meant to represent a definite traditional human type of eunuchoid characteristics, with short well-made arms and legs, and with small hands and feet, . . . generally shown naked, and . . . always without genitalia, sometimes wearing a simple loincloth or a short skirt with an ornamental buckle in front. The strong feline feeling always prevails and is coupled with an infantile character and expression about the faces, as if . . . to represent a totemic prototype, half jaguar and half baby. One type of sculpture undoubtedly represents a jaguar cub ancestor, as so often its snarling mouth shows the toothless gums of a newly born baby.

The Colossal Heads (Fig. 30) show no such jaguar ad-mixture and lack the tiger mouth. They do conform to the Olmec aesthetic ideal, however, in that all are plump, snub-nosed, thick lipped, and helmeted. They very well might be memorial portraits of rulers.

Feline features are also lacking in dwarfs (Fig. 23). These often display deformities: a hunched back, a club foot, no lower jaw. Covarrubias (1957: 57) supposes them to be *chaneques*, impish dwarfs which have survived in Mexican folklore.

Realistic jaguars almost never appear in Olmec art; rather, felines are highly stylized (Fig. 20). This is consistent with the general aim of Olmec art away from realism.

Nevertheless, the technical skills for realistic depiction were brought into play in the Colossal Heads. Kubler (1962: chart, p. xxxiii) sees these as a late development within the Olmec style. If the Colossal Heads are indeed portraits, they can be thought of as reflections of late developments within Olmec society as well. Surely a high degree of social differentiation would have to have come about before portraits of individuals could be produced. Like landscape, realistic portraiture is un-known in the art of primitive societies. Only with the begin-nings of civilization and its concomitant social stratification do certain individuals literally "stand out." These prominent per-sonages, upon whom society depends for its direction, are im-mortalized in the creations of their followers. The realism of portraiture in no way is inconsistent with stylization of non-human forms; non-human forms show no individuality in the world of the artist.

The human-jaguar combinations in Olmec art could be of totemic origin. The anthropological concept of totems covers a wide range of beliefs about mystical relationships between human kinship units and specific animals, plants, or other natural phenomena. Today, the Maya still cling to such beliefs (Holland 1961). Universally, people living within a clan or-ganization hold that they are descended from a primordial non-human ancestor.

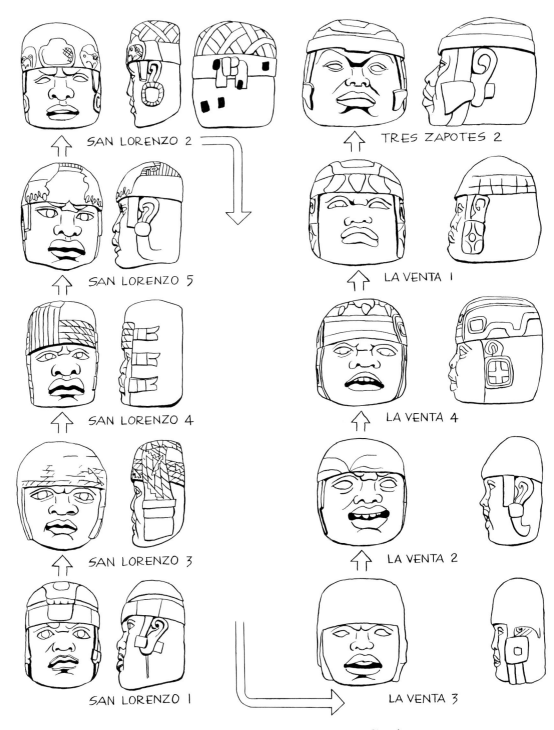

Fig. 30. Colossal Heads with arrows indicating
the chronology of their development.

The massive fragments of sculpture found by Stirling (1955) in the Río Chiquito area indicate that the Olmecs held the jaguar as a totemic ancestor. Monument 1 from Río Chiquito (Fig. 19) and Monument 3 from Potrero Nuevo (Fig. 22) are alike, 1) in depicting a jaguar on top of a human as if engaged in sexual intercourse, and 2) in being wrecked. A puritanical orientation of some alien group that invaded in Precolumbian times could explain the fragmentation, just as puritanism in Postcolumbian times prevented a realistic description of the sculpture in the *National Geographic*. Puritanism is shown to have existed outside of Western history by a reading of the *Popol Vuh* and the *Chilam Balam*. These ancient Maya texts rage against the sexual permissiveness of latter-day invaders from central Mexico. Their militant tone should alert us to the possibility of the Maya's having been responsible for the destruction of the Río Chiquito statues.

The sexual union celebrated in stone was certainly celebrated in myth as well. The most likely inference from the human-feline representations is that they spring from mythology which told of a totemic ancestor: a mighty jaguar. Indeed, the destroyers of these sculptures might not have been puritanical zealots, but rather ideological fanatics, literally myth-smashers.

The "Concept" of the Subject.

Kubler (1962a: 66) sees "two sharply contrasting modes of sculpture" in the Olmec. One, which "approaches cipher-like abstraction," he calls the "ideographic mode" because of its similarity to glyphic notation. Examples are the mosaic floor, sarcophagus, and Altar 1 from La Venta, and the tiger mask on Stela C from Tres Zapotes (Figs. 15, 31). The other mode Kubler calls "veristic" by which he means the "most faithful possible transposition of appearances." The Colossal Heads and the wrestler from the Corona collection exemplify the veristic mode (Figs. 30, 32). Apparently Kubler considers the modes as antipodal with most Olmec sculpture ranging between.

Fig. 31. Altar 1, La Venta, Tabasco

As we have mentioned, one likely intention of the creators of the veristic Colossal Heads was realistic portraiture of specific personages. An imposing look was generally incorporated with the likeness. Facial expression combined with the large size in the Colossal Heads to produce a commanding presence. One of the Colossal Heads is over nine feet tall; three are over eight (Kubler 1962a: 67, f.n. 11). Nor is massiveness limited to the Heads: Stelae 2 and 3 at La Venta measure around 11 feet high (Covarrubias 1957: 67-68) (Figs. 7, 9).

As with all art created with the purpose of inspiring awe, the principle of frontality, although not in its extreme or total form, is expressed in monumental Olmec sculpture. This is perhaps most obvious in Altars 4 and 5 from La Venta, which show a large central figure facing out of a deep arched niche (Figs. 8, 16). With few exceptions, partial frontality is the rule in surface carving.

Fig. 32. The Wrestler

Hauser (1957: 41) could very well have been describing Olmec reliefs when he set forth the devices of frontality in general. The chest is always turned to the viewer —

so that the upper part of the body is divisible by a vertical line into two equal halves. This axial approach, offering the broadest possible view of the body, obviously attempts to present the clearest and least complicated impression possible, in order to prevent any misunderstanding, confusion, or concealment of the elements of the picture. The attribution of frontality to a basic lack of technical skill may be justified to some extent, but the stubborn retention of this technique, even in periods in which there can no longer be any question of such an involuntary limitation of artistic purpose, demands another explanation.

In the frontal representation of the human figure, the forward turning of the upper part of the body is the expression of a definite and direct relationship to the onlooker . . . .

In Olmec reliefs the head is always presented in profile. The forward-looking central figure of La Venta Stela 2 (Fig. 7) cannot be considered an exception as it is in such high relief as to be sculpture in the round. Feet are shown in profile and pointed in the same direction unless the figure is in repose. The moving leg is usually the rear one as is the farthest-reaching arm.

For Hauser (1957: 41) "All courtly and courteous art, intent on bestowing fame and praise, contains an element of the principle of frontality — of confronting the onlooker . . . " There can be little doubt that the leaders of the La Venta center sought to overwhelm both visiting pilgrims, and perhaps viewers yet unborn, with the idea of their might.

Technical Form.

Because he was a particularly sensitive artist, Miguel Covarrubias (1957: 54) has given us perhaps the best analysis of the forms utilized by the Olmec sculptor.

"Olmec" art is the very antithesis of the formalized and rigid art of the highlands or the flamboyant baroque of the lowlands of the Classic period, both overburdened with religious symbolism and ceremonial functionalism. On the other hand, its aesthetic ideology is in the spirit of the early cultures: simplicity and sensual realism of form, vigorous and original conceptions. The "Olmec" artists . . . handled . . . forms with architectural discipline and sensitivity. They delighted in the smooth, highly polished surfaces of their jades, broken occasionally by fine incised lines to indicate such supplementary elements as tattooing, details of dress, ornaments, and angular shapes with rounded corners . . . .

"Architectonic" is perhaps the best one-word characterization of Olmec sculptural form. The Olmec altars resemble a rectangular house form. Olmec jade figurines could be called streamlined; indeed, their curved and highly polished surfaces are reminiscent of the modern automobile, and the incised lines that break the surfaces seem to serve the same artistic function as the fine lines of chrome that accent the polished surface of the products of Detroit.

Summary

The foregoing breakdown of Olmec art follows a tripartite scheme developed by the anthropologist A. L. Kroeber. The artist-anthropologist Miguel Covarrubias was extensively quoted in the characterization although he did not knowingly follow Kroeber in writing on ancient Mesoamerican styles. The ideas of art historians George Kubler and Arnold Hauser have also been drawn upon. I trust that this demonstrates in a small way that the anthropologist and the art historian are not at cross purposes. Far from being mutually exclusive, their approaches reinforce one another. Principally, I have tried to set forth Kroeber's anthropological approach to style by applying it to the specific case of the Olmec.

The anthropological approach is so broad that it can handle the art of any people living or extinct. Anthropology focusses on the role played by culture or tradition in art production. Moreover, anthropology generally deals with the art of societies rather than with that of individuals.

An analogy can be drawn between art and what anthropologists have learned of language: both have styles; both evolve, in part, through "drift." Techniques worked out by anthropologists for the study of languages might bear fruit, then, if applied to the study of styles. For example, an art style, like a language, can be viewed as a configuration or it can be segmented into components. The application of Kroeber's three levels to Olmec style demonstrates how this can be done in art studies. In addition, the example provides the reader with an overview of the Olmec style.

3

Inferences from Olmec Art and Archaeology

THE ONLY EVIDENCE AVAILABLE for making inferences about Olmec society is the art and architecture of a long vanished people. Inferences never come from a direct confrontation with the evidence, however; they are the result of observing the evidence through the screen of theory.

In the choice of theoretical tools with which to unravel the problem of the nature of Olmec society, I must admit that I have been outlandishly eclectic. To excuse myself partially I point out that anthropology is a young science lacking the solid body of theory of her older sisters, e.g., astronomy and chemistry.

By combining theories from several fields, we are able to see the creators of Olmec art in several contexts. After viewing them thus we can ask whether what is implied in one theoretical context is consistent with that of another. Consistencies of inference should be assuring; jarring antitheses should lead to reconsiderations.

Ethnology, archaeology, sociology, economics, and psychology all have the behavior of man as their central concern. Perhaps each can tell us something about the particular men that interest us at the moment: the creators of Olmec art. In this hope, I have brought together such unlikely bedfellows as Robert Redfield, Pitirim Sorokin, Karl Marx, Emile Durkheim, and Sigmund Freud. I trust that the analogy holds that while one plank cannot stand alone, several leaned toward one another can soar high above the ground.

In the previous chapter I inferred from the size, subject matter, and partial frontality of Olmec monumental sculpture the presence of a dominant social class. At the same time, I have treated Olmec monuments as if they were merely museum pieces. Yet Olmec art has an archaeological context from which its social context can be inferred. Art in the isolation of a museum can tell us little about its creators; only within a social context can it be fully understood.

What is intrinsic to art that makes it either primitive or civilized? In answering this question we are confronted with the realization that much of what we label primitive art is so named because of what we know of its origins. Little is intrinsically primitive about any piece of art. "Primitive art is the art of primitive societies," says one definition. This is not so tautological as might seem at first glance. Ethnologists, who study primitive societies, have collected much of the primitive art on display in the world's museums. They have given us a social context whereby we can call a piece of art primitive. Indeed, ethnographic accounts often attempt to show the relationship of art to society. Let us look, for a moment, at one ethnologist's theoretical approach to the problem of such relationships.

The Redfield Continuum

Phillip H. Lewis (1961: 236), a curator of primitive art, tacitly admits that his subject matter can only be defined as the art produced by societies considered as typologically primitive. According to Lewis, an art object can be classified as primitive only if its provenience — its original social context — is roughly known. The problem is not to define an object as primitive *per se*, but to define a society as primitive. For a characterization of primitive society Lewis has seized upon Robert Redfield's theoretical typology. Redfield (1953: 12, 22) pictures societal types as located along a continuum between idealized extreme forms. At the antipodes are primitive or precivilized society and urban society.

The primitive and precivilized communities are held together essentially by common understandings as to the ultimate nature and purpose of life. The precivilized society was like the present-day primitive society in [these] characteristics [of] isolation, smallness, homogeneity, persistence in the common effort to make a way of living under relatively stable circumstances . . .

Whereas:

. . . a society is civilized insofar as the community is no longer small, isolated, homogeneous and self-sufficient; as the division of labor is no longer simple; as impersonal relationships come to take the place of personal relationships; as familial connections come to be modified or supplanted by those of political affiliation or contract; and as thinking has become reflective and systematic.

Although obviously useful to the museum curator working with "ethnographic art," can Redfield's construct help the archaeologist who deals with art of long vanished peoples? Because the archaeologist encounters physical contexts rather than social ones, his difficulties are greater than those of the ethnologist confronted by a living group. The archaeologist can say little about the "common understandings as to the ultimate nature and purpose of life" of those who populated an ancient settlement. What the archaeologist can do is determine how small and isolated a community may have been. Furthermore, he might be able to make inferences about the homogeneity of the ideas of a people from the homogeneity of their artifacts.

The Beardsley Series

In contrast to Redfield's continuum, the classification of cultures developed by Richard K. Beardsley and others (1956) is suited to archaeological as well as to ethnographic contexts. At the same time, both schemes show polarities which go from rural to urban.

Only one criterion — community mobility — differentiates societies in the Beardsley series. A group of anthropologists, under Beardsley's chairmanship, directed their joint efforts at creating a classification that could be used by both ethnologists and archaeologists. In this they were successful. The series they elaborated can be considered to fit within a continuum, and in this it approaches Redfield's construct. In fixing upon only one criterion, however, it contrasts markedly.

Each member of the series is a "community pattern" defined as "the organization of economic, socio-political, and ceremonial interrelationships within a community, and is largely synonymous with 'culture complex' " (p. 134).

If we follow Drucker and Heizer's (1960) interpretation of the archaeological finds at La Venta, the Olmec community pattern there can be no other than Differentially Simple Nuclear Centered. This means that a permanent community serves as a point around which several less stable villages are organized. The qualifier "Differentially" is prefixed to show that the permanent center is qualitatively, as well as quantitatively, at variance with its satellites. In the case of the La Venta center — the only one that is well known up to now — the ceremonial nature is undeniable. In this way La Venta was set apart from her satellites.

The Beardsley group assumed that archaeological cultures can be compared with ethnographic cultures. (The same assumption lies behind the training in anthropology that archaeologists receive in the Americas.) Consequently, from archaeological data inferences are possible that have "functional and evolutionary as well as historical and descriptive significance" (Beardsley and others 1956: 133). In comparing the community pattern for La Venta, as demonstrated by archaeological research, with that of ethnographically known cultures, specific inferences are forthcoming. The Simple Nuclear Centered pattern reveals full-time occupational specialization typically based on heredity and social stratification, and, at the same time, many social groups based on kinship.

The chief acts to some extent in his own interest or the interest of his class, and usually has power to coerce subjects, particularly as individuals or as members of the lower class. His power is related to the size and distinctness of the upper class . . . . Individuals or families of high status tend to live . . . in the permanent center in a differentiated [community] . . . . Religion is formalized and externalized in temples, ritual, prayers, and offerings. Sacrifice becomes a means of influencing the gods. A ceremonial calendar determines the time of ceremonies. Both increase in community size and specialization of religious ritual seem to be responsible for the allocation of part of the community to an audience role rather than the participation characteristic in Semi-Permanent Sedentary and in Wandering groups. Public ceremonies directed toward community goals (successful harvest, rainfall, victory over enemies, etc.) predominate over those commemorating births, puberty, and death. Gods become differentiated from ghosts and spirits, and priests from shamans. Ceremonial paraphernalia are elaborated. [p. 142]

An undercurrent of evolutionary thinking churns below the language of this citation. Yet nothing in the characterization is at variance with the archaeological findings at La Venta. The Olmec center in the Gulf Coast region reflects a new way of life in Mesoamerica: birth and death of the individual are no longer public concerns; ceremonies of the agricultural community reflect preoccupation with bountiful harvests and victorious skirmishes. La Venta seems the product of an extremely dynamic period in Mesoamerican history.

However, we need not accept this picture as a faithful delineation of the Olmec on the basis of this particular typology alone. Other theories bear on the problem. Let us now consider some of these relevant constructs to see how they support the Beardsley plank of our formulation.

Sorokin's Polar Types

The sociologist Pitirim A. Sorokin relates art forms to social forms. After a study of Sorokin's theories, the anthropologist A. L. Kroeber concluded that they could be incorporated with Redfield's folk-urban continuum. Specifically Kroeber (1963: 179) thought that the dichotomy of Ideational and Sensate forms of art described by Sorokin mirrors Redfield's antipodes: Ideational forms reflect the rural condition, and Sensate the urban.

What does Sorokin mean by Ideational and Sensate? Sorokin has done no less than order the art production of all time. The art of any age will fit somewhere between his polar types of Ideational and Sensate.

Ideational art is that which transforms the invisible world into visible signs. It is transcendental. At its purest, it represents supersensory or superempirical subjects such as gods or spirits. In its impure form, it endows superempirical concepts with a visual resemblance as was done, for example, in depicting the familiar allegorical figure of justice blindfolded and grasping a balance. On the other hand, the subject itself may be empirical but depicted in a symbolic way as in the geometric designs on North American Indian pots which symbolize animals. In general, the style of Ideational art is linear and the subject matter static.

Sensate or visual art is antipodal to Ideational. Exemplified by impressionistic painting, its aim is realism. Because it is illusionary or empirical, a painterly style is suited to it. Painterly style (the *malerish* of Wölfflin) contrasts in its soft or blurred edges with the hard linearity of Ideational art. Again, being illusionary, it depicts movement of things in nature.

Along the continuum lying between Ideational and Sensate art there crystalizes fairly close to Ideational art a category which, in the main, conforms to Olmec art. This is Sorokin's Idealistic. Greek art of the fifth century B.C. exemplifies it. It depicts not empirical reality, but an ideal form of reality. Individual fancy, so characteristic of the visual impressionists, has no place here. The earthly is ignored. Its figures are eternal and static, calm and serene. Lasting, traditional values are sought. Idealistic art differs from Ideational in having connections with the empirical and it differs from visual in that the empirical is limited to idealized traditional themes.

... The nonidealistic phenomena ... are out of place in such an art. *It passes by the prosaic, the debased, the defective, the common, the earthly.* It does not see the baby as a baby, the old man as senile, the woman as womanish; what it sees is some general and perfected type of man. Therefore its babies are grown up; its old men are youthful; its women are manly — there is no sex in them. [Sorokin 1962: Vol. 1, 260]

This passage brings to mind the grown-up looking babies on the sides of Altar 5 at La Venta (Fig. 16) and the rather sexless adults who hold them; are they masculine women or womanly males? Probably they represent, like the three-dimensional figure within the niche that holds a child, the perfected type of male. A definite female on Stela 1 from La Venta (Fig. 5) despite being bare-breasted, is about as sensuous as cold porridge. Yet she is serene.

Again, the Colossal Heads (Fig. 30) show a sexless serenity. Universally they are thought to represent males, but from their appearance one would have difficulty proving it. Indeed, in noting the similarity of their helmets with that of the headgear on the female of Stela 1, Ignacio Bernal (personal communication) presents an enigma. Could the Colossal Heads be representations of women? Personally, I am inclined to view them as perfected males. The monumentality of the heads would have been lost had they been carved from blocks of the same size, but with tall headdresses like those of the men on the Chalcatzingo reliefs (Fig. 11).

From what social milieu spring these serene Olmec monuments? Sorokin (p. 258-59) believes that Idealistic art is nurtured by specific social circumstances.

> Since the Idealistic art has behind it, as its inspiration and soul, some great ideal, such an ideal or value is always the value of a genuine collectivity. It is not, and cannot be mere individual fancy. It is logical, therefore, to expect that this value embraces within itself the collectivity in which the individual artists are only the leaders. Everybody strives to contribute what he can to such creation because the value is the common value of all. Hence the art of such periods tends to be stamped by the collective character of its individual artists. In this sense it is *nonindividualistic, collectivistic,* or *"familistic".*

> ... Idealistic art ... has been in considerable degree the work of the aristocracy and nobility, great, chivalrous, noble, and idealistic, whether hereditary or not, whether in the form of the great Greeks who readily sacrificed themselves for the glory of gods and country at Marathon or elsewhere, or in the form of the feudal aristocracy at its apex. [p. 683]

In the previous chapter a consideration of the content of Olmec art led us to postulate a dominant social stratum in Olmec society. Now we see that Sorokin infers an aristocracy or nobility from Idealistic art. Again, this is the same inference that Beardsley and his group draw from the Simple Nuclear Centered settlement pattern shown by La Venta. They speak of "individuals or families of high status."

In the Beardsley scheme the aristocracy is responsible for the construction of the differentiated center upon which surrounding villages depend. The chief even possesses "power to coerce subjects" and so can direct them in the transport of building materials and construction. For Sorokin it is the noble patrons who demand that art depict them in an idealistic or perfected form. And they hold the power to do this.

Coincidentally, in fitting the Olmec settlement pattern of the La Venta region into Beardsley's scheme and the content of Olmec art into Sorokin's, in neither case are the examples polar. In each they lie along their respective continua, seemingly closer to the rural end than to the urban. Admittedly, some subjectivism enters into this judgment. Beardsley does not claim that the steps along his continuum are equal, and Sorokin's Idealistic type is *any* mixture of Ideational and Sensate.

Marx: Economics and Art

The ideas of Karl Marx on the relation of art to society lack the exactness that we see in Sorokin. The problem never appears central in Marx's writings. Marx makes passing references to it in letters or mentions it in formal writings as an aspect of some larger problem. Marx did write a great deal about the concept of work, however. Therefore, theoreticians wishing to discover the Marxian dogma of art have reasoned that since art production is a form of work, what Marx said about work applies as well to art (e.g., Ernst Fischer 1963: pp. 15 ff.).

Even if this is correct, we are still left with concepts difficult to use in a study of a specific society and its art. Marx's generalities in themselves, however, can be stimulating and suggestive. Without adhering to the Marxian view of the primacy of the economic factor, anthropologists would allow that all aspects of culture — including social organization and art — are interrelated. Indeed, it is the manner of this interrelation that poses most of the problem-oriented research of anthropology. What, then, were Marx's views about interrelationships of art and society?

According to the Marxist dialectic, history is a struggle between opposing tendencies of thesis and antithesis which become resolved on an ever higher level. Marx saw the material world as the ultimate reality, ideas being merely a reflection of it; Sorokin's view is just the opposite. For Marx the omnipresent conflict which makes historical development occurs between social classes. Owners of the means of production must defend their wealth and privileges from those who produce. Shifts in economic control are keys to historical change, and can be abrupt or revolutionary since those in power do not often voluntarily relinquish their position.

Upon socio-economic factors, according to Marx, lies a superstructure which includes the rest of culture. Art styles are included within the superstructure and are responsive to the socio-economic milieu. Art styles usually reflect, directly or indirectly, the interests of the ruling class. Thus a radical change in the dominant art style, seen in an archaeological context, as between adjoining strata, would likely reflect a social upheaval.

At the same time, elements of earlier styles can persist under conditions of change.

> Marxism emphasizes the role of environment, especially the socio-economic environment, in determining the main characteristics of art. Changes in it, as in the case of a revolution which redistributes wealth and power, tend to change all forms of cultural expression. The type and quality of art at any time are not due to supernatural inspiration or to innate racial superiority. Social conditions can provide themes and general direction to art, but there is always room for individual variation. They do not determine the specific details of a period or individual style. The precise ways in which genius will treat common themes can not be predicted or explained by purely socio-economic factors. But social conditions can release and inspire creativity, or the opposite. [Munro 1963: 97]

Although Marxian theory has attempted to relate art to society, it has done so — as the above citation makes clear — only in very general terms. A consequence of this lack of specificity shows up in the writings of latter-day Marxists. For example, Miguel Covarrubias' views on the socio-political significance of Olmec art reflect this vagueness.

The type of society of a vanished people can be determined by the character and personality of its archaeological remains. In the case of the "Olmecs," only an aristocracy obsessed with a rather fossilized religion and hunger for self-glorification and having unlimited resources of labor could have accomplished the carving and erection of such great monuments, and particularly the transportation of enormous masses of basalt into an area so totally devoid of stone as the alluvial plains of the Isthmus. Two basic human types are often shown in "Olmec" art, perhaps corresponding to two different social classes of people who lived together: the squat, dwarfish, flat-nosed personages — vassals; and the refined, aquiline, and often bearded people — the elite. Furthermore, at Tlatilco the remains of the simple pottery-making peasants of Zacatenco culture are found together with elaborate "Olmec" objects, indicating that the early agriculturalists came in contact with a more complex, urban type of people, shamans or magicians who in time became the intellectual masters, taking the first step toward the establishment of an aristocracy, a parasitic class of priests, and thus prepared the stage for the great theocracies of the subsequent period. [Covarrubias 1957: 77]

Covarrubias sees evidence of a class war merely because two differing physical types are depicted in Olmec art. Certainly this is grasping at Marxian straws. The flat-nosed personages are held to be vassals, yet the majestic Colossal Heads are all flat-nosed. In one instance, on the Stela from Alvarado, Veracruz, a smooth-faced, flat-nosed person is shown in a position subservient to a bearded, aquiline-nosed figure. But this is merely one instance. In the Chalcatzingo reliefs (Fig. 11) a bearded personage is shown nude and tied at the wrists.

Again, the phrase "parasitic class" smacks of Marxian oversimplification. The concept of a leisure class was not elaborated by Marx, however, but by Thorstein Veblen, and given wide currency by Veblen's *The Theory of the Leisure Class* (1899). Despite the title, Veblen's pronouncements in this work cannot be taken as generalities that hold for all societies. As Mills (1959: 58 f.n.) has pointed out, *The Theory of the Leisure Class* is merely a theory of one element of the upper class in one epoch in the history of one country.

To dismiss the Olmec elite, as Covarrubias has done, as a "parasitic class" seems unwarranted. The upper class must

have contained the thinkers and the organizers of Olmec society. Far from being idle, its members directed the production
of public works and public art. "Saprophytic" fits them better
than "parasitic."

The significance of Marx's writings lies not in the catch
phrases gleaned from them, but rather in opening our eyes
wider to the understanding of history. In part because of
Marx's indirect influence, few modern, non-Marxist anthropologists or historians would argue that an inquiry into the means
of production of a society is not essential for an understanding
of that society.

A most penetrating inquiry into Olmec modes of production and economic organization has been made by Robert
Heizer. Struck by the enormous expenditure of work represented by the ruins of La Venta, Heizer calculated the man-
hours required in assembling materials and the making of
"mammoth offerings," pyramids, and monuments. La Venta
impressed him as a manifestation of the emergence of a theocratic state. "The La Venta site, by reason of its age, isolated
position, and restricted population-support area, constitutes
the earliest specific example of a Preclassic priest-dominated
society maintaining a major ceremonial center" (Heizer 1960:
221; cf. Heizer 1961, Drucker 1961).

Heizer inferred that the area administered by La Venta
was that adjoining the coast between the Coatzacoalcos and
Tonalá rivers: a 350-square-mile topographic region of low hills
with an estimated population of 18,000 (Heizer 1960: 219).
The economy of this area was based on the production of maize
using slash-and-burn agriculture. Heizer follows Boas, Childe,
Kroeber, and Wolf in observing that plant domestication was
truly revolutionary since it allowed for the "production of surplus foods, and heavier populations which had more free time
available which might be diverted into non-subsistence activities and from which could develop specialization of skills"
(Heizer 1960: 215). At the same time Heizer notes that the

delicate ecological balance between population and available land can be easily upset under the conditions of the *milpa* system.

The importance of efficient agricultural production to the development of complex society has long been recognized by Marxists. Lewis Henry Morgan's *Ancient Society* (1877), which greatly influenced Marx and Engels, contains the embryonic idea of the importance of surplus production. The concept has been elaborated by later scholars. Recently, however, the anthropological theorist Marvin Harris pointed out a fallacy within it, of utmost importance to our understanding of the Olmec. Harris says that the concept of surplus production goes against the basic evolutionary tenent that reproductive potential is superior to productive ability. Population explosion is but the current expression of this doctrine.

The belief that specialization and stratification arise when the labor force produces more food than it needs cannot be reconciled with the fact that, largely as a result of malnutrition, the majority of the world's food producers have never survived beyond infancy or early adulthood. This malnutrition does not arise from a failure of the people concerned to provide themselves with enough energy to meet the demands of the minimum thermodynamic subsistence level, but rather from a failure to meet the additional requirements imposed by the sociocultural order, foremost among which are reproduction, the support of immature workers, and the support of a large nonfood-producing class.

Those who believe that a class of nonfood-producers arose when the food producers had produced more than they or their offspring needed for their own metabolic balance must show how neither the birth rate, death rate, abortion, infanticide, nor emigration of food producers was influenced by food shortages over an extended period of time. [Harris 1959: 191–92]

Human beings are fertile enough to reproduce themselves five and six times over at each generation; a normal couple can have ten or twelve offspring. For agricultural production to increase five or six fold with each generation is not so easy.

How is this significant to our attempt to make inferences about the economy of the Olmecs? It certainly means that we cannot rule out the possibility that a majority of the Olmecs suffered from endemic malnutrition because of the supremacy of reproductive potential over productive ability. Yet we know from both historical and current examples that this would not have precluded the channeling of their efforts into nonsubsistence activities. We may assume that an elite of non-agriculturalists planned and directed the building of the ceremonial centers in the Olmec heartland. What is not answered in this assumption is the vital question of just how the elite brought this about. How were they able to convince the agriculturalist to part with a share of this produce even in the face of endemic starvation? How was he induced to support the building of a site like La Venta? What methods did the Olmec leaders select from a spectrum that graduated from friendly persuasion to coercion?

Of relevance in answering such questions are the estimates worked out by Heizer (1960, 1961) of the man-hours necessary for the construction of La Venta. First he notes that because rainfall is seasonal in the tropical lowlands of Mexico, agriculture can be practiced only part of the year. Therefore, the labor required for the assembly of materials and construction at La Venta would hardly have been applied at the expense of agricultural labor. Heizer's figure, admittedly highly conjectural, is on the order of 2 million man-days' work. Spread over the 400 years of the La Venta occupation this would involve only 50 men working every year during the 100-day dry season (Heizer 1961: 47). Evidence indicates that rather than being evenly distributed over the entire occupation span, the construction of La Venta was carried out in spurts. Nevertheless, the order of labor involved as calculated by Heizer seems far from the "unlimited resources" postulated by Covarrubias.

All this is not to deny that the invention of agriculture and the eventual rise of ceremonial or urban centers are related. We know that, whereas the practice of agriculture does not inevitably lead to civilization, civilization never forms without the economic underpinning of agriculture. Yet the widely held belief in a direct development from agriculture to civilization seems almost too simple. A complex interplay between technological growth and social change appears more likely in the emergence of a new way of life. Certainly changes in social structure can affect technological change as well as the reverse. The Marxian view, nonetheless, postulates the primacy of technological change in any transformation of society.

As we have mentioned, Marxian theory has served for more than an ideological rationale in power politics. It widened the vistas of historians to include economics. Today it is a commonplace that a significant description of an era includes its means of production and distribution. To accept this as obvious does not mean that the historian accepts economic determinism as well. Sorokin speaks of economic determinism this way:

> It is evident that such a conception cannot be accepted factually, such factors as geographical conditions and biological drives inherent in man appeared and operated earlier than the economic factors. Other social factors, such as intelligence, experience, religious ideas or superstitions, rules of taboo or *mores*, primitive art, activity devoted to what could be called ideal aims, play and so on, are found in the most primitive human societies known to us and operated as early as economic conditions.

Sorokin notes that Engels had second thoughts about Marx's view "that the economic factor is exclusively sufficient to explain all historical and social processes," and modified the role of the economic factor so that it became merely a principal factor. With this Engels did not escape all difficulty:

> Marx and Engels did not even attempt to give any method for measuring the importance or efficiency of various factors, neither did they give any indices of the "primacy" of the economic factor, nor any logical motivation of their claim. This is enough to contend that the pluralistic interpretation of the Marx-Engels theory strips it of any originality, and amounts to its abandonment. [Sorokin 1928: 536]

Class Conflict and Empire Building

Marx's widely disseminated views on class conflict as a force in history have likely influenced our inferences about the ancient monuments. Be the pyramids Egyptian or Mesoamerican, the gigantic works bring to the imagination scenes as in a spectacular film. Thousands of men, naked to the waist, tug at massive stone blocks under the grim stare of whip-bearing overseers. At the periphery of the wide screen, finely dressed members of the elite casually converse in the shade. But can we safely infer that the archaeological monuments were built by coercion? The anthropologist David Kaplan thinks not.

Kaplan (1963: 407) feels that Mesoamericanists generally have "overestimated the socio-political complexity of the pre-Hispanic cultures" by underestimating "the ability of many stateless societies, particularly chiefdoms, to engage in communal production on a fairly large scale." He argues that estimates, like Heizer's, of the number of man-hours involved in large-scale constructions are useless for inferring the requisite socio-political organization unless we can determine as well how the expenditure of labor was distributed over time. Thus, large public works need not necessarily imply complex coercive political systems.

Kaplan's "chiefdom" is

a societal type with a political organization headed by a permanent office which has authoritative regulation over several local groups or communities, but which does not have an effective centralized monopoly of force. The chiefdom contrasts with the state, which unites on a territorial basis a number of local groups under the authority of an office or set of offices, in which is vested effective, centralized monopoly of the use of force. [p. 400]

The ethnographic literature shows that although social stratification does occur in stateless societies, its ranking is based on kinship and geneological seniority and not on the accumulation of wealth. In such societies, the incentives for construction of public works lie not so much in coercion as in "the desire for public approval and prestige, duty to community, religious sentiment, pleasure and pride in community . . ." (Kaplan 1936: 402).

In holding that chiefdoms characterized *all* Mesoamerican societies, Kaplan may have been somewhat brash. True empires could have been an important social form in Classic and Post-classic times. However, I follow Kaplan in that archaeological evidence does not allow the inference of an empire for the Olmec or other peoples of the Preclassic. Data from the Olmec heartland and from the Formative and Early Classic periods all over Mesoamerica do not indicate to me coercive states or empires.

Opposing this view, the eminent Mexican archaeologist Alfonso Caso believes that one is justified in inferring an Olmec empire from archaeological evidence. For Caso, the widespread distribution of monumental Olmec art is indicative of a conquest state. However, the presence of a far-reaching style is not enough in itself from which to infer an empire; for Caso homogeneity of style is crucial as well. He feels that the occurrence of Olmec monumental style from northern Veracruz to El Salvador is analogous to the distribution of Roman art and architecture in the Old World. In both cases the styles vary little from place to place. In contrast to Roman, European Gothic art showed regional diversity as it diffused across political boundaries.

Admittedly, opinions about the homogeneity or heterogeneity of an art style are personal. One could well argue that outside the heartland the Olmec style differs from that within it. For example, Colossal Heads are not to be found outside a small circumference that bounds San Lorenzo, La Venta, and Tres Zapotes. Indeed, with the exception of one monument from eastern Morelos, no sculpture in the round appears outside the Olmec heartland. Reliefs far from the epicenter such as at Chalcatzingo, Morelos (Figs. 10 and 11) and Chalchuapa, El Salvador (Fig. 24), lack the extreme frontality of those heartland monuments which approach sculpture in the round such as Stela 2, La Venta (Fig. 7), and the numerous tabletop altars. Differences between peripheral and heartland Olmec art, therefore, appear to me — to return to Caso's analogy — like those between the Gothic of Ile de France and England. Unfortunately, such judgments cannot be measured in absolute terms, and their subjectivism renders them unscientific.

In disagreeing with Caso about the probability of an Olmec Empire, I do not wish to leave the impression that I hold that no empires existed in ancient Mexico. Historical accounts leave little doubt about an Aztec Empire, for example. Naturally, Caso (1963) is able to make a much better case for an Aztec Empire than for an Olmec Empire because data on the Aztec are more complete; the archaeological record is enriched by Spanish eye-witness accounts and the writings of native historians.

Indeed, the picture presented by sixteenth-century writings contrasts markedly with Kaplan's "chiefdom." Tenochtitlan, which the *conquistadores* compared to Venice, was certainly a true city. Its urbanites were organized not on a tribal or kinship basis, but according to the principle of coresidence. Nevertheless, Caso (1963) emphasizes that the city wards, called *calpulli*, might have ultimately rested on an ancient kinship-based organization: the clan. Evidence against this view is the absence of clans among groups linguistically related to the Aztec within the Uto-Aztecan language family.

The possibility of an ancient clan organization seems much greater for Maya, however. And it is to the Maya rather than to the Aztec that we must look as the direct heirs of Olmec culture. A possible survival indicating clan organization for the Maya has been found by William Holland (1964). In highland Chiapas the Tzotzil Maya of today practice ancestor worship. The Tzotzil believe that their social organization, structured along generational lines, has a double in the spirit world. Each Tzotzil possesses a counterpart in the form of a companion animal. The animal double of the person with the greatest political power in a Tzotzil community is thought to be a giant jaguar. This could be of importance for considerations of Olmec beliefs as reflected in art.

In our discussion of the objective subject matter of Olmec art, Covarrubias was quoted as seeing in jaguar representations a totemic ancestor figure. The statues from the Río Chiquito area (Figs. 19, 22), which show a jaguar copulating with a human, support this view. But what lies behind a people's view that they descend from a giant cat? Emile Durkheim, the great French sociologist, thought that totemism was of considerable theoretical importance. Perhaps a consideration of Durkheim's ideas on totemism in general will lead us to more inferences about the Olmec.

Durkheim, Totems, and the Jaguar People

Durkheim observed that no intrinsic quality of the totemic object is sufficient reason for the awe which it inspires. A social group "out of the commonest object, . . . can make a most powerful sacred being" (Durkheim 1961: 259). In bestowing the totemic aura upon the jaguar, the Olmecs did choose a being whose intrinsic qualities inspire fear, but, as Durkheim showed, *any* object made to function as a totem becomes imbued with qualities outside itself. In a word, it becomes sacred while other objects are profane.

In seeking the origin of the concept of sacredness, Durkheim utilized the data available to him from Spencer and Gillen's pioneer anthropological study of Australian aborigines. He contrasted the two distinct phases in the life of Australian societies. Usually the population becomes dispersed as small groups go about the humdrum work of gathering seeds, roots, and grubs, and of hunting and fishing. "The dispersed condition in which the society finds itself results in making its life uniform, languishing and dull" (Durkheim 1961: 246). In contrast to the monotony of subsistence activities, gatherings of a clan or tribe for ceremonies are exciting. At such times the individual is transformed outside himself. "The very fact of concentration acts as an exceptionally powerful stimulant. When they once come together, a sort of electricity is formed by their collecting which quickly transports them to an extraordinary degree of exaltation" (p. 247). The exaltation felt by the individual on these occasions, when contrasted with the lethargy engendered by ordinary pursuits, gives a sacred quality to everything that takes place at the ceremonial gatherings. Thus, according to Durkheim, the idea of sacredness has a social basis.

The totemic object can be the symbol of the clan or tribe or of whatever group comes together on sacred occasions. The object takes on a symbolic value which need have no relation to its intrinsic value. The symbolic value of the totem, then, is the result of the shared belief of the collectivity.

The behavior of the Australians, as interpreted by Durkheim, offers insight into the archaeological remains of La Venta and other Olmec centers and adds weight to Kaplan's view on the lack of coercion in pre-urban societies. The shifting cultivation of slash-and-burn tropical forest agriculture, presumably practiced by the Olmec, requires dispersed settlement and low population densities. For the system to work, the major part of the lands must lie fallow. The demographic effect of slash-and-burn agriculture has been termed by Wolf (1959: 60) "strongly centrifugal." This means that as families become large, new family units bud off to seek new lands. We would suppose that relatives so separated would want to see one another again. Furthermore the dry season, a slack time in agricultural work, would be the most convenient time for family reunions. Gradual budding off during a period of steadily increasing agricultural exploitation of the area between the Coatzacoalcos and the Tonalá rivers would conflict with the continuing desire of the inhabitants to reunite with kinsmen each year; the most logical solution would be to settle upon one location at which to reconvene. This is how the San Lorenzo and La Venta ceremonial centers could have come into being.

These speculations on the rise of the Olmec ceremonial centers should not be interpreted as economic or environmental determinism. Rather they can be considered as an example of what Julian Steward (1955: 36ff.) has called "cultural ecology," which "introduces the local environment as the extracultural factor in the fruitless assumption that culture comes from culture."

I do not wish to imply that the Olmec farmers can be compared with Australian hunters and gatherers except in a very general way. Like the Australian, the native of the Olmec region would have had a sacred time of the year to contrast with the humdrum period of work. During the sacred period, he probably left his hamlet and journeyed to the ceremonial center to unite with kinsmen. Over the years, however, in contrast to the Australian situation, population growth may have resulted in many of the ties of kin being forgotten and replaced by ties of group solidarity.

The jaguar, perhaps originally the symbol of a clan or of a tribe, became the sacred emblem of the group that convened at La Venta. The jaguar totem was worshipped because it had become the symbol of the collective itself. The Olmecs were, literally, what historian Wigberto Jiménez Moreno has called them: "Tenocelome," the people of the jaguar.

Motifs other than the jaguar are represented in the monumental stone sculpture at La Venta, however. Humans appear prominently. Who are they, and what was their relationship to the pilgrims who gathered at the ceremonial center? As the sculptures show, these were no ordinary mortals. Their majestic bearing reminds us of Durkheim's postulation that a group need not be limited to animals, plants, or inanimate objects in choosing a symbol of social solidarity:

. . . We see society constantly creating sacred things out of ordinary ones. If it happens to fall in love with a man and if it thinks it has found in him the principal aspirations that move it, as well as the means of satisfying them, this man will be raised above the others and, as it were, deified. Opinion will invest him with a majority exactly analogous to that protecting the gods . . . . The simple deference inspired by men invested with high social functions is not different in nature from religious respect. It is expressed by the same movements: a man keeps at a distance from a high personage; he approaches him only with precautions; in conversing with him, he uses other gestures and language than those used with ordinary mortals. The sentiment felt on these occasions is so closely related to the religious sentiment that many peoples have confounded the two. In order to explain the considerations accorded to princes, nobles and political chiefs, a sacred character has been attributed to them . . . . [Durkheim 1961: 243–44]

Quite possibly the men made larger than life in La Venta sculpture manifest the deification treated by Durkheim. Perhaps the apotheosis grew out of the veneration for patriarchs in earlier times. Ancestor worship could have been part of this complex. At La Venta the foremost priest-ruler could have kept his distance from the ordinary pilgrim to the extent that he appeared to him only in gigantic stone sculpture. The jaguar may have been at the same time both the totem of the Olmec group and the animal counterpart of their supreme leader.

Freud and the Psychological Factor

The Olmec leaders, whose visages in stone inspired awe in the collective, can be thought of in Freudian terms at the level of individual perception. In this context the term "authority figure" comes to mind. Sigmund Freud's theories do not conflict with Durkheim's. Rather they treat different levels of perception. In the same way Sorokin's ideas on the sociology of art or Marxian views on the economic factor in art are neither necessarily mutually exclusive nor contradictory. Art has a sociological as well as a psychological content.

Freudians view art much as they do dreams. Art can reflect repressed desires which have been frustrated in everyday life. Psychoanalysis shows "that art is not only a form of exposure, but also one of disguise, that works of art are created not only as forms of self-revelation and communication, but also as a means of concealment, self-deception, and deceit, or, at most, of confessing but half the truth" (Hauser 1963: 105).

To be completely understood, a work of art, then, must be explained not only in terms of what it proclaims to be, but of what it unconsciously is.

The Freudian interpretation would probably see in the emphasis on the tiger mouth in Olmec art a manifestation of the oral personality. From this it could be inferred that the typical or "modal" personality of the Olmec group was oral. Anxieties about eating are characteristic of the oral personality. Such attitudes appear in much of the surviving indigenous folklore of Mexico which seems blatantly oral in its fixation on eating.

However, little is accomplished by characterizing Olmec art as oral. It tells us about as much as the Freudians do in explaining "a social structure so extremely complex and historically intricate as capitalism by the simple and homogeneous proclivity to anal eroticism" (Hauser 1963: 105). It is too simplistic an explanation.

Further criticisms of Freud's theories are implicit in the work of anthropologists Malinowski and Mead. Much of what Freud considered universal does not exist where social structure differs markedly from that of late nineteenth-century Vienna. The Oedipus complex, emotional trauma in teen-agers, and inherent "female" mental traits are not found in all societies.

The application of Freud's ideas tells us little about the creators of Olmec art except that they probably suffered anxieties about eating. This meshes well with Harris's views of endemic hunger among food producers. But Freudian considerations of art leave us nothing specific.

Fischer's Socio-psychological Factor

Perhaps we have dismissed Freud in too cavalier a fashion. Certainly Freud's genius has had a profound role in shaping the twentieth-century view of man. The pervasive consequences of his writings can be compared only to those of Marx. His seminal works have inspired myriad schools of psychology.

Even in denouncing him, no psychologist is without debt to the master.

Social psychology was one of the many limbs to grow out of the trunk of Freudianism. Bent by the criticism of anthropologists, the branch aimed at consideration of the individual in reference to his culture and society. Since art is necessarily created by individuals within particular cultures and societies, it can be studied from the viewpoint of social psychology.

A fascinating pioneer application of social psychology to art analysis is that of J. L. Fischer. Fischer (1961) sought to relate art style and socio-cultural conditions by the use of psychological factors. His data were judgments on art styles made by psychologist Herbert Barry III and judgments on societies made by anthropologist George Murdock. Their decisions were arrived at independently, with no thought of being correlated.

Fischer's theory holds that an important causal factor in art forms is social fantasy as expressed by the artist. Social fantasy includes both the actual and desired situations of the society. From this, Fischer hypothesized that art reflects an egalitarian society to the extent that it is 1) repetitious, 2) spacious, 3) symmetrical, and 4) lacking in enclosed motifs.

Each hypothesis was examined by means of the (R. A.) Fischer-Yates test. This is a statistical measure of the correlation between two independent samples of small size where all samples fall into two mutually exclusive categories. An art style will feature repetition, empty space, symmetry, and enclosure, or it will not; a society can be egalitarian or not. In each case there exist two mutually exclusive categories about which to make a judgment. In the Fischer study in all cases where actual values were compared with expected random ones, the probability of there being no correlation was less than 5 per cent.

Fischer (1961: 90) remarks:

> For an anthropologist, one of the most exciting possibilities that the study of art styles and social conditions opens up is the application to extinct cultures known only through archaeology. If we can learn enough of the

pan-human implications of art styles for social structure and the resulting psychological processes, we should eventually be able to add a major new dimension to our reconstruction of the life of extinct peoples known only from their material remains.

This is a hopeful prospect, indeed. While granting that the millennium may be long in arriving, an application of Fischer's hypotheses (p. 81) to Olmec art should produce implications about the society that created it. In turn, these implications can be compared with the inferences that we have already made about Olmec society using other criteria.

Fischer's hypothesis 1

Design repetitive of a number of rather simple elements should characterize the egalitarian societies; design integrating a number of unlike elements should be characteristic of the hierarchical societies.

Examples of repetitive elements and of integrating designs can be cited for Olmec art. Egalitarian status seems to be implied by the plethora of identical stone figurines in private and museum collections. These are males with flattened, warped bodies which are nude or with a breechclout indicated by incision, but with never an indication of the sexual member. In proportion to the body, the head is high and it receives more attention from the artist. Whereas body and limbs are treated summarily, the head, always pear-shaped, always jutting forward from the chest, is detailed. The group of sixteen figures discovered by Drucker and Heizer (1956: photograph p. 366) at La Venta hints that the figures were used in depicting ceremonies or, perhaps, other events as we today use toy soldiers. Marching soldiers, all from the same mold, depict the egalitarian sector of an army rank-and-file. Olmec stone figurines appear somewhat analogous.

Furthermore, clay figurines constitute one of the most characteristic traits of the Preclassic. In the Valley of Mexico, where they have been most intensively studied, only a few basic types appear. Yet they are found by the thousands at all

Preclassic Valley sites. It is commonly assumed that these figurines of humble clay were produced by village-farming, egalitarian societies. According to Fischer's theory, they represent the artists' views of society.

In the graves at Tlatilco, in the Valley of Mexico, delicately fashioned clay figurines of Vaillant's "D" type are by far the most common. In this trait, Olmec-influenced Tlatilco contrasts with other Preclassic sites in the Valley which show more common types of figures. Could the "D" type figurines represent an idea shared by the elite at Tlatilco? Could the figures be counterparts of those who waited upon the elite in life and who, hopefully, would serve them after death?

If this be the *raison d'être* for the "D" figurines, servants were perceived by the Tlatilco elite as a mass from which individual differences did not emerge. But how were the elite pictured by those below them? The viewpoint seems to be embodied in Vaillant's type "A" figurines. Unlike the "D" type, these are widespread in Middle Preclassic sites throughout the Valley of Mexico and are even found in the La Venta area. Type "A" figurines show a characteristic gritty clay differing from the smooth clay of the other types in the Valley of Mexico and indicating that they were probably imports from the La Venta region. The physical type they represent is unmistakably that of the Colossal Heads of the Olmec heartland (Fig. 30) with thick lips, wide noses, and fat cheeks. In all probability the clay figurines were mass-produced by peasants. The peasant-eye view apparently has reduced the elite to a mass. A sociologist might describe the phenomenon causing this as "social distance." The figurines seem to show that social distance was by no means directed only one way in Olmec society.

Contrasting with the monotony of clay figurines is the variety of the monolithic works from the heartland area. In all likelihood, the works in stone were commissioned and directly supervised by the elite. Just as Philip IV retained Velázquez to immortalize the members of Spain's court, the

elite of La Venta employed sculptors whose names are unknown to us. It is not surprising that the art which most evinces
a hierarchical society is manifest in the Olmec heartland area.

Fischer's hypothesis 2

Design with a large amount of empty or irrelevant space should characterize the egalitarian societies; design with little irrelevant (empty) space
should characterize the hierarchical societies.

Olmec art cannot match the *horror vacui* manifest in
Maya reliefs. Personages on Maya stelae look out at us from
a baroque jungle of costuming. The headdress, almost as high
as the figure itself, is a totem-pole with head upon varied head
each with its own intricate headdress of feathers and jade. The
body is completely covered by elaborate cape, pectoral ornament, and breechclout. All that is visible of the human beneath
the finery are two hands that emerge to grasp a ceremonial bar
and the outpointing feet almost completely covered by high-
backed sandals. In turn, Maya relief tablets are packed with
glyphs which fill their otherwise empty spaces.

Were the Maya, therefore, more hierarchical than the
Olmec? We would suspect that they were because of their
centers, the content of their art, and their temporal relationship
to the Olmecs. Perhaps Maya art's showing almost no empty
space is another indication of a hierarchical society.

In Olmec art uncrowded reliefs like Monument 13 (Fig.
33) appear at La Venta along with crowded ones like Stelae 2
and 3 (Figs. 7, 9). According to the Fischer hypothesis this
reflects social conditions. One could order the reliefs from the
Olmec heartland relative to decreasing empty space. Would
this not indicate an increase in social stratification and be at
the same time a guide to the evolution of Olmec art?

Fischer's hypothesis 3

Symmetrical design (a special case of repetition) should characterize
the egalitarian societies; asymmetrical design should characterize the hierarchical societies.

Fig. 33. Monument 13, La Venta

Symmetrical design typifies Olmec art, but asymmetry also occurs. The bilateral symmetry of the Dwarf Altar, Monument 2, from Potrero Neuvo (Fig. 23) and the anthropomorphic jaguar, Monument 10, from San Lorenzo (Fig. 20) contrast with the asymmetry of Monuments 13 and 19 (Figs. 9, 25) from La Venta. There is but one inconsistency: the asymmetric Monument 13 shows much empty space while La Venta Stela 2 (Fig. 7) is symmetrical, but shows little empty space. Thus, in the same piece one criterion points to an egalitarian society while the other indicates a hierarchical one. This does not necessarily mean that Fischer is wrong. More likely it indicates a transition from the egalitarian tribal society of the past to the complex hierarchical society of classes or castes of the future.

Fischer's hypothesis 4

Figures without enclosures should characterize the egalitarian societies; enclosed figures should characterize the hierarchical societies.

An enclosure indicates that one is separated from the masses. In everyday life, physical devices operate to set leaders apart from the lower strata of society. Walls, guards, vehicles all operate in this way. The artist's unconscious reaction to devices is to show enclosures in his work. Certainly the figures enclosed by the niches of Olmec altars give every appearance of being from the top ranks of a hierarchy. In addition to their splendid isolation within the niche, their demeanor and dress establish this impression. At the same time, tabletop altars with niches show an overall bilaterally symmetrical design indicative of egalitarianism. This again points to Olmec society's being in transition.

The Colossal Heads were isolated by their very placement within the architectural complex of La Venta (Fig. 17). Following Fischer's hypothesis, this is a further indication that they can be none other than portraits of the rulers or directors of the Olmec centers.

Summary

Social and psychological theories have been brought to bear on the problem of the nature of Olmec society. The inferences which they have produced agree strikingly. Thus, Sorokin's social theory of art and Fischer's psychological one result in similar conclusions about the fabricators of Olmec art. Judged stylistically, Olmec monolithic works fall under Sorokin's rubric of Idealistic art. Sorokin's characterization of Idealistic art as "nonindividualistic" and "collectivistic" matches Fischer's "egalitarian." At the same time, both theories signal a hierarchical element in Olmec style. This, in turn, relates to the Marxian view that, in general, art style mirrors the concerns of the ruling class.

Since the ultimate origins of art cannot be other than socio-cultural and psychological, social and psychological theories of art production should agree. If valid, such theories will prove complementary, never contradictory.

Archaeological and environmental studies show La Venta as a ceremonial center surrounded by small agricultural settlements. In the Beardsley formulation the category Differentially Simple Nuclear Centered applies to the settlement pattern which lasted more than half a millennium at La Venta. Based on ethnographic parallels, the Beardsley scheme uses the term "chief" to specify the leader of the community type, and correlates perfectly with Kaplan's concept of "chiefdom" as a societal configuration in Mesoamerican cultures. Kaplan notes that the ties of kinship can be the basis for ranking in a chiefdom.

I have presented the view that kinship ties could have exerted as well a centripetal force to counter the centrifugal demographic effect of slash-and-burn agriculture as described by Heizer, Drucker, and Wolf. In the process, an explanation was extracted from Durkheim — the reunion desire in diffused kinship groups. Such reunions create a contagious excitement

— "electricity is formed" in Durkheim's words — so different from the bleakness of day-to-day living as to seem miraculous. The contrast is so stark that reunion appears sacred in contrast to the secular realm of ordinary pursuits.

I agree with Kaplan that in hypothesizing a coercive state to account for the ancient monuments and cities of Meso-america some authorities seem unduly influenced by recent history. In an age of coercion and secular religion it is easy to forget that solid evidence tells of an age whose hallmark was the true believer. Gothic cathedrals arose decade after decade not because of coercion, but because religion was a real force and men wished to create an image of heaven here on earth. Why else would the citizens of Chartres have piously pulled stone blocks to the cathedral site while their horses romped free in the meadow? That religious belief may seem non-rational does not lessen its importance as a motivating force in history.

To follow Kaplan's assertion that we underestimate what chiefdoms are capable of is necessarily to disagree with Caso, who upholds the possibility of an Olmec Empire. The societal type of chiefdom is far removed from that of the conquest state.

From the content of Olmec art was inferred a religion centering around ancestor worship and the jaguar totem. De-scriptions of ancestor worship and the belief in totems by con-temporary highland Maya Indians, set down by my late friend William Holland, were offered as supporting evidence for this view of ancient Olmec religious practices.

Marvin Harris's ideas on surplus were introduced to dem-onstrate that the concept of surplus production is inadequate to explain the flowering of civilization. Furthermore, Harris's critique leads us to the conclusion that even when faced with endemic hunger a people can expend their energies on the sacred sphere. Thereby they produce social surpluses dramati-cally at variance with their individual scarcities.

Along with less-known centers like San Lorenzo and Tres Zapotes, the site of La Venta is nothing less than the concrete remains of effort expended in the realm of religion. At La Venta generation after generation of peasant families living between the Coatzacoalcos and the Tonala rivers came together at regular intervals dictated by the annual agricultural cycle. They gathered to meet relatives and friends and to feel the excitement of joining in worship of their chief ancestors and the companion animal of these, the jaguar.

4

The Guttman Scale and Its Application to Olmec Style

IN THE PRECEDING CHAPTER, the application of both socio-cultural and psychological theories of art production to the specific problem of Olmec art shows the two positions to be neither contradictory nor mutually exclusive, but corroborative.

One inference has been that principal determinants of the content of Olmec art are socio-cultural: specifically the belief in revered ancestors and their jaguar guardian spirits. A second inference has been that psychological determinants led to certain aspects 6f the main themes, as in the isolation of human figures within a niche or the elaboration of the mouth in representations of jaguars.

[109]

Together, these two factors — the socio-cultural and the psychological — can account for the ultimate or primordial origins of art. The socio-cultural factor is the contribution of a particular society with a specific culture; the psychological, that of the individual artist. Obviously, the two factors overlap. Culture (the learned, shared behavior transmitted as the *traditions* of a society) contributes heavily to the formation of the individual personality. Despite this intimate relationship, it appears more promising for gaining insight into art production to treat the socio-cultural and psychological factors as separate entities.

The Stylistic Factor

Fortunately, it matters little for our immediate aims whether we consider socio-cultural and psychological factors separately or together. Whether we lump or split them, they can be set apart from the factor which we must isolate if we are to study the evolution of Olmec art. This remaining ingredient of art is the stylistic factor. The differentiation of the stylistic factor from others involved in producing a work of art has been set forth by Arnold Hauser (1963: 126):

. . . Besides the factors rooted in social reality or determined by the desire for self-expression, there is the whole apparatus of the craft, of instruments that are gradually and progressively perfected, as in any other technique. This apparatus has its own history, which *is* on the whole one of continuous progress attributable to immanent causation. Though the production of these instruments is not altogether independent of the general conditions of life, and is subject to interruptions and regressions, it is still quite reasonable to speak of an autonomous development here . . . . Even the formal and representational elements in art manifest certain intrinsic developmental trends independent of the circumstances and aims of the particular artist; such trends, however, are dominant only for a period and may at any time be reversed.

This, then, is that factor in art akin to linguistic drift. Each individual artist must necessarily confront the art production of the immediate past and leave his image upon it. Under an apprenticeship system, such a confrontation is so gradual that it might better be called a blending of artist with his art. It is characteristic of the rural society that its members are tradition-minded, that they do not ordinarily question the status quo. From this, it might be suspected that in a society like the Olmec, just emerging from its homogeneous state, there would be a strong sense of tradition among its artists. Consequently, the stylistic factor would be important to an analysis of Olmec art because significant changes could be observed within it.

Isolating the Stylistic Factor

How can the stylistic factor be isolated from the socio-cultural and psychological factors? In artistic change through time, the stylistic factor embraces those changes which are most regular and consistent. Only by ignoring novelties and exploring consistencies can the stylistic factor be exposed. Previous analytical studies in anthropology may point the way.

In their cleverly conceived study of changes in women's fashions, Richardson and Kroeber (1940) isolated the stylistic factor. They measured dimensions of women's dresses for the U.S. as recorded in catalogues for 150 years. Obviously a skirt becomes unwieldy beyond a certain width, and restricts movement when made narrow. Thus a skirt has to fluctuate in width between two dimensions. Other parts of dress must do the same.* When repeated or copied, any form can either gain, lose, or remain stable. With this, all logical possibilities are exhausted. What Richardson and Kroeber showed for several dimensions in dress was that such changes take place in a patterned manner. Changes in dress dimensions differ from our

---

*So must the measurements of an automobile. In the mid-1950s a shrinking of what were the longest and widest auto models was taking place because their unwieldiness had become too onerous to be compensated by owner feelings of prestige.

preconception of the world of *haute couture*. Not at all erratic, dress dimensions created a fifty-year fluctuation between the possible extremes in each, or in cycles of one century.

Richardson and Kroeber utilized date-bearing fashion magazines and catalogues for their study. Equally reliable dating was available to Tatiana Proskouriakoff (1950) for her ingenious study of patterns in Maya dress; dates in a relative chronology are carved on the same stelae that bear elaborately costumed personages. In contrast, except in rare instances, Olmec monuments show no dates. Exact chronological marks on individual pieces of sculpture are virtually unknown. Because of this lack of precise dating, the task of discovering the stylistic factor in Olmec art is more complex.

How, indeed, are we to solve it? In the Richardson and Kroeber and in the Proskouriakoff studies, data were first ordered chronologically. Only then were the patterned changes extracted from them. These changes were consistent over time. In both studies, several aspects of dress were demonstrated as evolving, each going its own, unvarying direction at the same time. If we were able to arrange pieces of Olmec sculpture in a way that would show several aspects altering in a regular manner, could we not assume that at the same time we have ordered them chronologically? In other words, we would be proceeding in just the reverse manner from the two pioneer studies of change. Just as the ordering of individual pieces in a relative chronology allowed earlier workers to isolate those elements undergoing consistent transformation, so would an ordering based on evolutionary patterns in style present a sequence with an underlying relative chronology. Stylistic fluctuation can only take place over time spans. A word of caution must be added, however: the determination of the top of the time scale offers difficulties and is a separate problem.

The inherent consistency and regularity of the stylistic factor distinguishes it from the socio-cultural and psychological factors of style. This difference not only sets the stylistic factor apart, but offers the possibility of its isolation. The discovery of the regular and consistent elements in an art style is the discovery of its stylistic factor. But how can such elements be detected?

Obviously, any group of objects can be arranged in relation to a single characteristic. For example, one physical dimension such as height can serve as a basis for such an arrangement. The ordering of objects in this way is called in statistical parlance "scaling." Any disparate group of a single object category (ships, sealing wax, cabbages, etc.) can be scaled according to one of its characteristics. But how can differences in one dimension be correlated with those in another? Can quantitative differences, as in height, be correlated with qualitative ones, as in color? How can such differences be interpreted as a function of the passage of time?

The Guttman Scale

Qualitative observations are essential to the analysis of art style. In some cases, quantitative observations as well may be important to analysis. By means of such observations sequences can emerge. Subjectivity in judgments of qualities is only one handicap of such observations; an even greater difficulty is that of treating many aspects, both qualitative and quantitative, at the same time. A way out of this dilemma is offered by a statistical procedure outlined in 1944 by Louis Guttman. Developed by Guttman and his associates for the purpose of investigating the morale of U.S. forces in World War II, it has since been applied widely in the field of sociology (Freeman and Winch 1957). Only recently have anthropologists begun to apply it to specific problems (Goodenough 1956, 1963; Carneiro and Tobias 1963).

Successful application of the Guttman analysis results in the ordering of qualitative or quantitative data into a configuration called a "scalogram." If data can be so ordered, they are inferred to be the expression of a single underlying variable. Conversely, data that result from several variables cannot be scaled.

Theoretically, the stylistic factor in art is determined by a single underlying variable: the evolution of style. Changes in any art style or "stylistic drift" make up the stylistic factor. It is because a single variable is involved that the method of Guttman scaling has been selected from a number of statistical tests. It should reveal just how Olmec style evolves. Because most Olmec monuments were not excavated carefully, and because they lack telling associations, they cannot be placed in an evolutionary sequence using archaeological inference alone.

The Guttman method can tell us what are the elements of style which change in stylistic drift. Implicit in "drift" is the passage of time. Only through time can the expression or function of stylistic drift be observed. Thus any Guttman scale constructed of the elements of Olmec style and accounted for by stylistic drift, will be an expression showing steps in artistic change over time.

Up to now, however, sociologists have generally employed Guttman scaling to uncover synchronic, or momentary, variables such as general attitudes. In contrast to such studies, the recent application of the Guttman scale by Robert Carneiro constitutes an intellectual breakthrough in that it reveals a variable expressed over time, or diachronic variable. Guttman scaling has led Carneiro (1962; Carneiro and Tobias 1963) to postulate a general evolution through unilinear stages for *all* societies.

Our scope is much more limited than that of Carneiro, but, like his, it is diachronic. We focus not on mankind as a whole, but on a single art style left to us presumably by a single culture. Therefore, any sequence that we may derive probably will have no meaning for the evolution of art styles generally.

Kubler's Sequence for Olmec Heads

One of the basic uses of Guttman scale analysis is to check the validity of a hypothesis holding that several items are the expression of a single underlying variable (Goodenough 1963: 240). A hypothesis about Olmec art that lends itself to such testing has been set forth by art historian George Kubler (1962a: 67). He feels that the Colossal Heads of the Olmec heartland show a definite developmental sequence:

The ten heads show a clear development through two, and possibly three, generations of sculptors, working with stone tools, repeating the same theme with increasing skill and power. Two heads are almost spherical, and nearly devoid of animation: Tres Zapotes and La Venta 1. The first seems arbitrarily rotund, with the features protected from accident by the beetling projection of the helmet across the brow and along the cheeks. The eyes are rimmed with heavy borders, and the eyeballs have an extremely convex curvature. The ears are abstract ciphers. The expression is grim and hard, without the supple modelling of all the other heads. La Venta 1 is also spherical, but the helmet meets the face in a less harsh line. The modelling of lips and eyes, though puffy, is more vivacious.

A second group of four is distinguished by parted lips, communicating an expression of speaking animation. Two in this group are spherical, and two are long-headed. The long heads (La Venta 3 and San Lorenzo 2) are more lively than the round heads (La Venta 2 and 4). La Venta 3 has deeply shadowed eyes and lips, suggestive of emotional tension, as in Greek sculpture under the influence of Scopas. The round heads (La Venta 2 and 4) are perhaps more animated in the open mouths, but the total effect of an inner emotional state is less apparent.

The final group consists only of heads from San Lorenzo (Nos. 1, 3, 4, 5). Only San Lorenzo 3 is round-headed. All four have the iris incised upon the eyeball, in a commanding expression of focused gaze. All are like idealized portraits expressed in firm flesh, heavy muscles, and articulated profiles. An effect of majestic will power and discipline is achieved by studied proportions and contours, in a composition of idealized physiognomic parts.

This sequence places round heads of grim aspect earlier than long heads of majestic expression. The intermediate group of long heads and round heads is characterized by parted lips. Tres Zapotes antedates La Venta, and San Lorenzo is terminal in the sequence.

Inadvertently, Kubler has overlooked the Colossal Head now in the plaza at Santiago Tuxtla, Veracruz, but which had probably originated in Tres Zapotes (Smith 1963: 128). The inclusion of Tres Zapotes 2 seemingly would not alter Kubler's formulation since it appears similar in all respects to the earlier-known Tres Zapotes head. Since Kubler wrote, the natives of San Lorenzo have turned up another head (Avelera 1965). As of 1966, although uncovered, the head remained in the earth, which unfortunately prevents us from having a good look at it. The find brings the total of Colossal Heads to an even dozen: two from Tres Zapotes, four from La Venta, and six from San Lorenzo. By no means should this be considered a final count; in all likelihood others lie buried in the Gulf Coast rain forests.

Kubler (1962a: 67 fn. 12) acknowledges that his hypothesis "rests only upon analogy with similar changes elsewhere, as in Greek pediment sculpture of c. 550–450 B.C., or early Gothic portal figures in northern France of c. 1140–1250." The feasibility of such an analogy strains the credulity of Heizer (personal communication), and such skepticism would probably be encountered among many other New World specialists. Therefore, I propose to test the Kubler hypothesis by statistical means.

In sociological applications of the Guttman scale, populations under study typically are representative samples of well-defined groups of people: male college students in Texas, infantry combat veterans of the North African campaign, Negro teachers in Manhattan high schools.

For statistical studies a population need not consist of people, however. A statistical "population" may be defined as "a complete set of objects" (Guttman 1944: 141).

In the present case our population consists of all of the Olmec Colossal Heads known archaeologically. Since others may be discovered, it may be argued that those now known comprise a true random sample of all Colossal Heads.

Our "statistical universe" theoretically takes in a complete set of the attributes of our objects. Such attributes may show any degree, or none, of correlation. This range is expressed statistically as zero (no correlation) to one or unity (complete correlation). We are not interested in all of the attributes of the Colossal Heads, however. Rather we wish to test for the three attributes which Kubler feels show a unitary correlation: facial expression, head-shape, and eye-type. Implicit in Kubler's statement is that the factor underlying this correlation is a regular and consistent stylistic change through time.

The Guttman Scale Applied to Kubler's Sequence

Just what is a Guttman scale? How does one go about the process of "scaling"? How can one interpret the results? We have avoided answering these questions because the clearest way to explain Guttman scaling is through example. Let us go about scaling the Colossal Heads.

As a first step in setting up a Guttman scale we may extract from Kubler's statement, quoted above, the essential attributes of the Colossal Heads and put them in tabular form. A plus (+) sign indicates the presence of an attribute, and a minus (−) its absence. (It should be noted that non-anthropologist Kubler does not intend by the term "long-headed" to mean dolichocephalic, but rather a long or rectangular face as opposed to a round one.) The characteristics we list are those he holds as being later than their complements (Table 1).

TABLE 1.

Kubler's Characterization of Olmec Colossal Heads

Traits   *Colossal Heads*

	Tres Zapotes	La Venta 1	La Venta 3	San Lorenzo 2	La Venta 2	La Venta 4	San Lorenzo 1	San Lorenzo 3	San Lorenzo 4	San Lorenzo 5
Long-headedness	−	−	+	+	−	−	+	−	+	+
Well-defined iris	−	−	−	−	−	−	+	+	+	+
Animation	−	−	+	+	+	−	−	+	+	+

Objectivity has been sought by adhering strictly to Kubler's characterization of the Colossal Heads. (Kubler certainly was not thinking of scalograms when he wrote of this possible sequence.) The heads and their traits are set down in the order that Kubler has mentioned them. This is not random ordering, however, since he is speaking in general terms of a chronological sequence.

According to the Guttman procedure, the information extracted from Kubler in tabular form (Table 1) must be rearranged for scaling. A scalogram results if a table can be rearranged to reveal a certain pattern. Two rules must be followed in this rearranging: (1) the most common attribute is placed at the top and the least common at the bottom with the others placed between them in order of their frequency and (2) the objects posessing the least attributes are moved to the left and those showing the most to the right. The two shifts when applied to the data in Table 1 result in the patterned configuration of Table 2.

The regrouping of the pluses and minuses manifests a definite pattern with the sole exception of one minus for long-headedness for San Lorenzo 3. The data have been scaled. This has resulted in a "scalogram." The characteristics of a scalogram in which no item is out of place are described by Carneiro (1962: 153):

This pattern has the appearance of a regular set of stair-steps and constitutes what is known as a *perfect scale*. If a set of items plotted against a sample of units from some population can be made to arrange themselves in this way by following the aforementioned rules, that set of items is said to be *scalable*. If a set of items cannot be made to assume this stair-step pattern — or a reasonably close approximation to it — those items are not scalable. It must not be thought that the emergence of a scale is simply an artifact of manipulation. Scaling as an attribute is either inherent in the data or it is not. Rearrangement . . . according to the stipulated rules merely brings it out; it does not and cannot create it.

While Carneiro (1962) seems to be the first to see the diachronic implications of scalograms, the present study appears to be the first application of the Guttman scale to the problem of stylistic evolution. Its value in analysis of change in art seems both promising and limitless.

Refinement of the Sequence

I have endeavored to refine Kubler's sequence through the employment of more objective criteria in Guttman scaling. For this I used an almost complete set of photographs showing each of the Colossal Heads full-face and in profile. Each was photographed with the same lens from approximately the same distance. The only head I was unable to photograph was Tres Zapotes 1. (A front view of Tres Zapotes 1 was substituted from Stirling 1939: 185.)

The gross dimensions of the heads appeared too capricious to offer any promise for scaling. This makes sense because the size of available blocks might well have been beyond the sculptor's control. Whereas the gross size of individual heads seemingly lacked significance, their *proportions* appeared to be meaningful.

In order to test this supposition the head in each photograph — both full-face and profile — was enlarged to a standard size. From the enlarged pictures three measurements were

TABLE 2.

Scalogram Ordering of Kubler's Characterization

Traits   *Colossal Heads*

	Tres Zapotes	La Venta 1	La Venta 2	La Venta 4	La Venta 3	San Lorenzo 2	San Lorenzo 3	San Lorenzo 1	San Lorenzo 4	San Lorenzo 5
Animation	−	−	+	+	+	+	+	+	+	+
Long-headedness	−	−	−	−	+	+	−	+	+	+
Well-defined iris	−	−	−	−	−	−	+	+	+	+

taken of each head: height, depth, and width. Slight adjust-
ments were made for photographs not directly full-face. Because of the aberrant shape of San Lorenzo 3 — wide temples,
narrow chin — no measurement of width was obtained. From
these figures, two indices were calculated: the width of each
head in relation to its height (h/w) and depth in relation to
height (h/d). The resulting ratios are given in Table 3.

TABLE 3.

Ratios of Olmec Colossal Heads

Colossal Head	Height/Width Ratio	Height/Depth Ratio
Tres Zapotes 1	1.10	—
Tres Zapotes 2	0.99	0.82
La Venta 1	0.92	1.05
La Venta 2	1.24	1.57
La Venta 3	1.27	1.70
La Venta 4	1.20	1.26
San Lorenzo 1	1.40	2.30
San Lorenzo 2	1.51	1.80
San Lorenzo 3	—	1.71
San Lorenzo 4	1.47	1.56
San Lorenzo 5	1.28	1.49

The numerical expression obtained for each h/w ratio
and for each h/d ratio is called an x value. The relationships
among the x values of the h/w ratios may be visualized by
plotting them along a straight line. The line functions as a
yardstick showing the range of variation. Ranging between
the highest and lowest value, the remaining h/w values are
set down on the line at distances in proportion to their numerical distance from the ends:

0.92	0.99	1.10	1.20	1.27	1.40	1.51
			1.24	1.28		1.47

Placed in this manner along a straight line, the h/w values are seen to form three clusters. Guided by these clusters, the line is divided into three segments or intervals. Each segment constitutes what may be called a y variable:

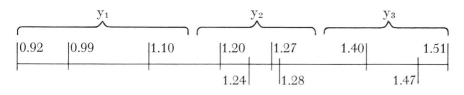

It is observed that these divisions are not equal intervals as on a calibrated scale. The y variables need not be equal intervals. Every x value is seen to be smaller than any x value within the y interval to the right of its own. Each y variable is said to be a single valued function of the x variable. This means that for each variable x there corresponds a single value of y. At the same time, for the same value of y there can be two or more values of x. In other words, if m is the number of our y values and n the number of our x values, we must satisfy the condition in making a scale that m is equal to, or less than n ($m \leq n$).

The interval y_1 includes all values below 1.15, y_2 embraces those from 1.16 to 1.33, and y_3 those above 1.34. Since $m = 3$ and $n = 10$ the condition $m \leq n$ is satisfied.

The numbers in the height/depth column of Table 3 may be plotted along a line in the same manner. This line, too, can be split into three divisions which follow the clustering of values along the line:

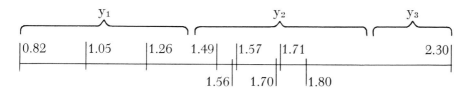

Here the intervals are: $y_1 = 0.82\text{-}1.40$, $y_2 = 1.41\text{-}2.00$, and $y_3 = 2.01\text{-}2.30$.

Calling the intervals y_1, y_2, and y_3 is arbitrary. They could just as well be tagged A, B, and C or X, Y, and Z. The same symbols are used for the divisions of all the continua described here purely for reasons of convenience. Just as the same symbols of plus and minus were used to characterize all of the items in Tables 1 and 2, and present use of the same symbols is merely to better observe the pattern of the resulting scalograms.

In this manner, qualities of relative proportion — wide vs. narrow, and deep vs. shallow — have been quantified and plotted along lines. Nevertheless, qualities do not necessarily have to be measured in order to be so plotted. Qualities that do not lend themselves to quantification may be scaled even though they have no numerical values.

As an example, consider the quality of facial expression of the Colossal Heads. Kubler theorized that the expression shown by the Colossal Heads evolved as did that of heads in Greek pediment sculpture and Gothic portal figures. The manner of the evolution supposed by Kubler also can be illustrated by plotting along a straight line. Instead of numbers, as in the case of proportions, the qualities themselves may be plotted. The straight line employed in this way may be thought of as the expression of a continuum, just as those along which were plotted degrees of height/width and height/depth. An analogy illustrates this: in a transformation in expression from grim to serene, or vice versa, the face undergoes a continuous action that can be recorded on motion-picture film. The strip of film may be thought of as a continuum of expression because along it are recorded all those minute changes involved in the facial alteration. So, too, the line along which the different expressions of the Colossal Heads are plotted may be thought of as a continuum.

As with the preceding linear representations, the points of

division are fairly arbitrary. Following Kubler's characterization of the facial expression of the Colossal Heads, the continuum represented by a line is divided into three segments: heads devoid of animation, heads with parted lips in speaking animation, and those of commanding or majestic expression. For the purpose of scaling, values of y_1, y_2, and y_3 respectively, may be assigned to these expressions.

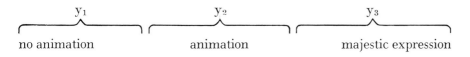

no animation   animation   majestic expression

A further quality of the Colossal Heads emphasized by Kubler is eye type. The heads may be divided on this basis and plotted along a line as with varying expression. Our photographs show what I consider three legitimate types: eyes without an iris, those with a slight indication of an iris, and those with the iris manifestly apparent. These types are tagged y_1, y_2, and y_3, respectively. As Kubler notes, his final group of four heads from San Lorenzo shows the iris. My observations are that, in addition, San Lorenzo 2 and the La Venta heads show the iris although not as patently as San Lorenzo 1, 3, 4, and 5. Because of its worn condition, La Venta 3 cannot be appraised. Once more, y values may be assigned to the graduations as follows:

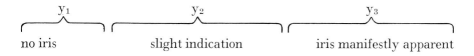

no iris   slight indication   iris manifestly apparent

Four items, then, are hypothesized as showing evolutionary changes within the stylistic factor: width, depth, facial expression, and iris indication. The y values assigned for each

TABLE 4.

The Refined Characterization of Olmec Colossal Heads

Traits	Colossal Heads										
	Tres Zapotes 1	Tres Zapotes 2	La Venta 1	La Venta 2	La Venta 3	La Venta 4	San Lorenzo 1	San Lorenzo 2	San Lorenzo 3	San Lorenzo 4	San Lorenzo 5
Width	y_1	y_1	y_1	y_2	y_2	y_2	y_3	y_3	?	y_3	y_3
Depth	—	y_1	y_1	y_2	y_2	y_1	y_3	y_2	y_2	y_2	y_2
Facial expression	y_1	y_1	y_1	y_2	y_2	y_2	y_3	y_2	y_3	y_3	y_3
Iris indication	y_1	y_1	y_2	y_2	—	y_2	y_3	y_2	y_3	y_3	y_3

item in each Colossal Head are tabulated in Table 4. The heads are set down in the random order in which they were discovered archaeologically.

For Guttman scaling the table must be rearranged according to the rules already applied to the more simple example. In this instance, heads with the most y_1 ratings are moved to the left, and those with the y_3 ratings to the right, with the y_2 ratings between. The y items themselves are rearranged so that the item with the most y_1's is at the top and that with the most y_3's is at the bottom. The two shifts applied to the data of Table 4 show that inherent in them is "scalability." The result of our manipulations is the scalogram shown in Table 5.

Table 5 shows a perfect scale: all y categories form solid blocks and the characteristic stairstep pattern emerges between the blocks of y_2's and y_3's. The conformation demonstrates that the features tested do not occur randomly. On the contrary, they are patterned and, therefore, meaningful.

Of what significance is the scalability of certain aspects of the Colossal Heads? My inference is that the scale is the expression of a sequential development. Changes indicated are changes within what we have set apart as the stylistic factor. The order of the heads in Table 5 is a chronological one.

The question remains as to which end of the series is closer in time to the present. Scaling alone cannot show us "which end is up." Kubler holds that serene expression is encountered in Greek and Gothic art only after some development and that, therefore, this end is later in the Olmec Heads.

Nevertheless, development in art is not always progressive. Degenerative processes also occur. The animal art of the Paleolithic cave paintings is richer than that of the Neolithic. The human figure is rendered more skillfully by the fifth-century B.C. Greeks than by the Romans whose control, in turn, was superior to that of the early Christians.

My original inclination in drawing conclusions from the scaling of the Colossal Heads was to follow Kubler's lead and say that the heads from Tres Zapotes come earliest followed by those from La Venta and San Lorenzo. Recent evidence opposes this formulation, however. Of the three sites, Michael Coe places San Lorenzo as earliest. Of six radiocarbon samples discovered in association with Olmec monoliths at the site in 1966, five give dates which fall within the 1200-850 B.C. bracket (M. Coe, personal communication).

This would place San Lorenzo at the end of the Lower Preclassic and before the La Venta florescence dated in Middle Preclassic between 800 and 400 B.C. by Drucker, Heizer, and

TABLE 5.

Scalogram Ordering of the Refined Characterization

Traits   *Colossal Heads*

	Tres Zapotes 1	Tres Zapotes 2	La Venta 1	La Venta 4	La Venta 2	La Venta 3	San Lorenzo 2	San Lorenzo 5	San Lorenzo 4	San Lorenzo 3	San Lorenzo 1
Depth	—	y_1	y_1	y_1	y_2	y_2	y_2	y_2	y_2	y_2	y_3
Facial expression	y_1	y_1	y_1	y_2	y_2	y_2	y_2	y_3	y_3	y_3	y_3
Iris indication	y_1	y_1	y_2	y_2	y_2	—	y_2	y_3	y_3	y_3	y_3
Width	y_1	y_1	y_1	y_2	y_2	y_2	y_3	y_2	y_3	?	y_3

Squire (1959). Tres Zapotes, although beginning in Middle Preclassic around 500 B.C., would continue into the Upper Preclassic (300 B.C. - A.D. 200?), according to Coe. Particular stone monuments from Tres Zapotes support this view. Monument C (Fig. 2) appears late stylistically because of its baroqueness. Stela C bears a bar-and-dot date interpreted as 31 B.C. in the Goodman-Martínez-Thompson correlation and as 291 B.C. in the Spinden correlation. Both dates fall within the Upper Preclassic.

In reversing my opinion to favor Coe's view as against Kubler's, I do not disagree with evidence offered by the scalogram itself. All that the scalogram can indicate is that a sequence is present for Colossal Heads from the three sites. It cannot tell us that one end is later and the other earlier. According to the scalogram, nonetheless, the La Venta Heads *must* come between those of the other two sites. In this Kubler and Coe agree with each other and with the scalogram. Coe's chronological data are convincing enough to lead us to favor the San Lorenzo, La Venta, Tres Zapotes ordering.

Perhaps one factor that influenced Kubler is the preservation of the San Lorenzo Heads which is better than those heads from La Venta. The considerable wearing of the La Venta Heads prejudices us almost unconsciously into thinking of them as older. Nevertheless, the better preservation of the San Lorenzo Heads cannot be admitted as evidence since all were rolled down into a ravine in ancient times and thus were better protected than the La Venta Heads which were left *in situ*.

A look at the heads arranged in the order of the scalogram evinces decreasing skill in the modeling of facial plains, lips, and helmets as one goes from the lower to the presumed upper end. In Fig. 30 only Tres Zapotes 1 and the newly discovered San Lorenzo 6 are not shown; both lie uncovered, but still in the earth. The head presumed earliest in the diagram, San Lorenzo 1, shows at the bottom left of Fig. 30 and the latest,

Tres Zapotes 2, at the top right. Full faces are flanked by profile views. The back of San Lorenzo 2 is presented to show its curious niches obviously added later.*

If one follows the sequence visually, the sensation is one of flow. Nothing jars the eye. The profiles become ever more deep, the lips more relaxed. The impression is of a tradition. The configuration or *gestalt* seems to confirm subjectively what has been shown analytically. The sequence is meaningful to both mind and eye.

The Ordering of Olmec Votive Axes

Marshall H. Saville's (1929) original grouping of several votive axes as being stylistically related led directly to the concept of the Olmec style. It may be assumed that Saville's basis for so classifying the axes was, in part, impressionistic. The axes show enough internal consistency in their stylistic features to be treated as an entity. Nevertheless, they lack the degree of homogeneity of the Colossal Heads. A further difference is that the provenience of the individual axes, where known, indicates they are found in a much more extensive area than are the heads.

This does not necessarily mean that the axes were manufactured over a wide area; they are small enough to have been easily transported for trade. Nevertheless, the possibility of dispersed manufacture must be considered along with that of a longer time range to account for the greater diversity of the axes in relation to the Colossal Heads.

More votive axes have become known since Saville's time. I have collected illustrations of eighteen as compared with the

---

*The purpose served by the niches is unknown. Perhaps a later people placed tenoned heads there of a form like the so-called "*hachas*" found on the Gulf Coast in Classic times. Parallels for this exist in the Old World as, for example, at Hellenistic Palmyra where columns show niches into which were set the tenons of consoles carved with the faces of rulers.

eight that he showed. The wider range of axes when joined with the technique of Guttman scale analysis permits the checking and refinement of Saville's original assemblage.

Table 6 lists the axes that are analyzed. The first eight are those of Saville in the order in which he described them. The names should be considered merely as tags although in most cases they do indicate the present whereabouts of the individual specimens. The order of the list is random except for Saville's obvious choice of describing first the two most striking pieces.

All apparent features of the axes were tested for scalability. Some possibilities could have been overlooked because of a lack of ingenuity. Each observed trait was manipulated in the manner of those features scaled for the Colossal Heads. Those which yielded scales were considered significant in demon-

TABLE 6.

List of Olmec Votive Axes

1. Kuntz (in American Museum of Natural History)
2. British Museum
3. Museum of American Indian
4. Dorenberg (in American Museum of Natural History)
5. Peabody Museum
6. Beyer (first published by Hermann Beyer)
7. Museo Nacional de México
8. U.S. National Museum
9. Covarrubias Collection (from Guerrero)
10. Cleveland Museum
11. Ekholm (from a photograph in possession of Gordon Ekholm)
12. Brummer Gallery
13. Museum of Villahermosa, Tabasco
14. Stendahl Gallery
15. La Venta (in Museo Nacional de México)
16. Covarrubias Collection — 2
17. U.S. National Museum — 2
18. Museum of Primitive Art

TABLE 7.

Characteristics of Olmec Votive Axes

Traits	1	2	3	4	5	6	7	8	9	10	11	12	13	14	15	16	17	18
Hand position	C	A	C	A	B	A	A	A	C	B	B	A	A	A	B	B	B	C
Mouth	B	A	B	A	B	A	A	A	B	B	B	A	A	A	A	B	B	B
Head form	B	A	B	A	B	A	A	A	B	B	B	B	A	A	A	B	A	B
Silhouette	B	B	B	B	B	A	A	A	B	B	B	A	A	A	B	B	B	B

strating an underlying variable. For every meaningful trait retained, many capricious ones were tested and discarded.

Two sets of items emerged from the testing. The first group scaled consists of the following features: whether mouth shows gums or fangs, presence or absence of a V-slit visible from front down center of head, and whether the entire specimen is of a rectangular or of an egg-shape form. These characteristics are indicated, for the purpose of manipulation, by having a letter stand for each: *position of hands* — A, in front on same level; B, no hands or hands on side; C, in front right above left; *mouth* — A, gums; B, fangs; *head form* — A, bifurcate (V-slit); B, non-bifurcate; *silhouette* — A, rectangular; B, egg-shaped. As in the scaling of the Colossal Heads, the symbols are used for each category merely to better illustrate the manner of their clustering in the scalogram. These characteristics can best be shown for each votive axe in tabular form (Table 7).

Regrouping of the axes so that those with the most A's are placed on the left side and those with the most B's and C's are on the right gives a scalogram (Table 8).

TABLE 8.

Scalogram Ordering of Olmec Votive Axes

Traits	14	13	6	8	7	2	12	15	4	17	16	11	10	5	18	9	3	1
Hand position	A	A	A	A	A	A	A	B	A	B	B	B	B	B	C	C	C	C
Mouth	A	A	A	A	A	A	A	A	A	B	B	B	B	B	B	B	B	B
Head form	A	A	A	A	A	A	B	A	B	A	B	B	B	B	B	B	B	B
Silhouette	A	A	A	A	A	B	A	B	B	B	B	B	B	B	B	B	B	B

Is the underlying variable which allowed the scaling of these traits the same evolutionary causal factor that was inferred for the Colossal Heads? I think not. Rather, by their very nature the traits are ones that would lead me to infer other than an evolutionary causal factor. The way they divide within the scalogram seems to indicate a difference in kind. What originally appeared to us as a single entity of Olmec axes may have constituted two for the artists that fashioned them.

Following this reasoning, I have made two groups of the axes by dividing the scalogram between numbers 4 and 17, the point in the scalogram at which the cleavage is greatest between the A's and B's. This results in an equal division of the 18 axes; all to the left show gums, those to the right, fangs. The axes exhibiting hands in front view are also divided by a line running vertically between numbers 4 and 17 into hands at the same level on the left and hands one above the other to the right. Head form and silhouette offer a few exceptions, which prevent the scalogram from being a perfect one.

Although scalograms are a new phenomenon and there is much to learn of their use, it is doubtful that perfection should be expected in the analysis of so complex a phenomenon as an art style. That configurations appear approaching perfection as in the present case seems significant, if not miraculous, to one who has tried the experiment suggested by Carneiro (1963: 198) of "filling out a matrix in some random way, such as by tossing a coin, and then seeing how much scaling can be made to appear."

TABLE 9

Second Scalogram Ordering of Votive Axes

Traits	9	4	11	14	12	5	18	3	10	8	13	7	15	1	2	6	16	17
Hand type	A	A	—	B	B	—	B	?	—	B	C	—	—	C	C	C	—	—
Fangs	A	—	A	—	—	B	B	B	B	—	—	—	—	C	—	—	C	C
Treatment above eye	—	A	A	A	A	—	—	A	A	B	A	B	B	—	B	?	?	?

The second group of traits emerged because it formed a separate and distinct scalogram. The items making up the group with their designations are: *hand type* — A, blocky hands without fingers; B, blocky hands with fingers; C, shaped hands with thumb indicated; *fangs* — A, straight; B, curved; C, double; *treatment above eye* — A, band; B, serrated plaque. These traits, when ordered in the same way as the previous example, give a scalogram (Table 9).

Again, an almost perfect scalogram has resulted; the data fit into a stairstep pattern, contrasting with the divisionary pattern of the previous scale. Because of the stairstep pattern and because of the nature of the traits that lend themselves to it, I have inferred that in scaling the axes an evolutionary sequence emerges.

The two scalograms for the traits of Olmec axes allow for the arrangement of axes shown in Fig. 34. The vertical division has been made on the basis of the first scalogram. It is the separation into what appears to be two kinds of axes fashioned by Olmec artisans: on the right are adult jaguars showing fangs and on the left infants with gums and the notch at the center of the head that might indicate the fontanel. The horizontal divisions follow the second scalogram. They reflect temporal differences.

The manner of the inferred evolution of the axes can be seen by comparing the diagram in Fig. 34 with Table 9. The configurations abstracted through Guttman scaling are graphically illustrated in Fig. 34. For example, axes D and E show the change from the square-fingered hand to the shaped-thumbed hand (E) as well as the progression from the band above the eye (E) to the serrated eye plaque (D).

Temporal evolution is inferred as the underlying factor here because each of the traits that comes into play shows a separate and independent development. The differences among each trait scaled are differences in degree of fang curvature or elaboration of hands. The change from block hands with no fingers to shaped ones with thumbs and from curved to double fangs is cumulative. In contrast, the division of votive axes into two distinct groups was done on the basis of differences in kind between ways or representing particular features, e.g., fangs as opposed to gums. To account for differences in degree we infer evolution; for differences in kind, separate entities.

The inference for temporal ordering in the sequence rests upon more than the idea of cumulation. A second principle that aids in understanding and explaining the evolutionary sequence is functional prerequisiteness. Carneiro (1962: 160–61) describes it:

> This principle amounts to something more than the familiar concept of functional dependence, which states merely that x depends on y, and y depends on x, in some reciprocal and synchronic manner. Functional prerequisiteness implies that x *necessarily precedes* y, which is to say that y cannot come into existence without the prior existence of x. Note that the principle does not state that y must follow x. It may and it may not.

The configuration of each of the traits of the axes placed uppermost in Fig. 34 seems to have developed out of configurations of axes lower in the inferred sequences. Thus the lower patterns hold a functional prerequisiteness for the upper ones. The traits placed highest in the diagram are held to be latest in time.

The question of how much time is involved in the evolution of the votive axes cannot be answered by scaling alone. Only a relative chronology can be inferred. Still the time span represented by stylistic changes in the votive axes seems much longer than that of the Colossal Head sequence; the changes in the votive axes are obviously much more radical than those of the head sequence.

Implications of the Sequences

Both the sequence for Colossal Heads and that for votive axes achieved by Guttman scaling are significant to the study of the Olmec. Let us consider the implications of each.

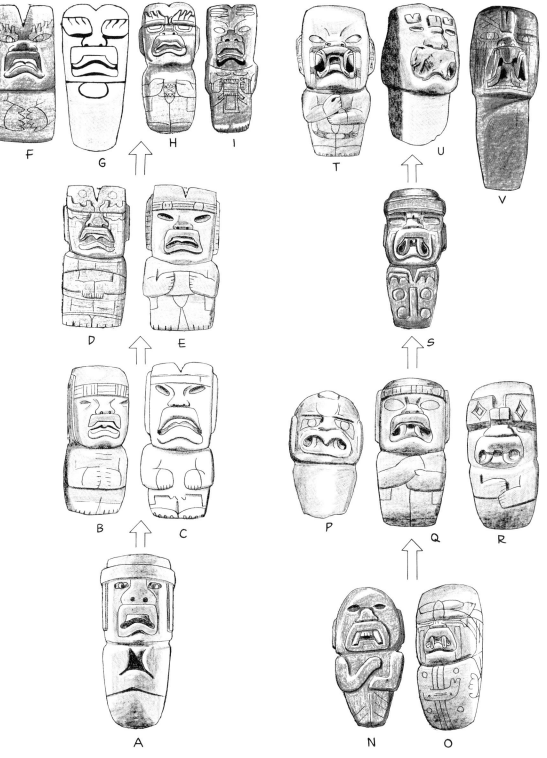

Fig. 34. Votive Axes with arrows indicating the chronology of their development

Colossal Heads come from Tres Zapotes, La Venta, and San Lorenzo. Within the Guttman scalogram, the heads are scaled according to origin so that those from San Lorenzo would appear to be earlier than those from La Venta and those from La Venta earlier than those from Tres Zapotes. Aside from this inference is the postulation that the heads represent portraits of supreme chieftain rulers. If this be true, it might indicate that the center of political power in the Olmec region shifted respectively from San Lorenzo to La Venta to Tres Zapotes.

Within the architectonic context of the site of La Venta the spatial pattern of the Colossal Heads correlates with the order of the heads in the scalogram. The map of La Venta (Fig. 17) shows Head 1, inferred as latest, isolated near the center line south of the large pyramid. Numbers 3, 2, and 4 are set in line north of the stone column enclosure from east to west in the same order that they appear in the scalogram. Thus it appears that this is most likely the order in which they were created and set up. Unfortunately, the monuments of San Lorenzo have been uprooted and rolled out of context so we can never know their original situation. Where spatial arrangements are preserved as at La Venta, I think that they may be profitably compared with similar configurations at Maya sites, about which more is known. This possibility is explored in the following chapter.

Summary

The statistical technique of Guttman scaling has been successfully applied to the analysis of art style for what is thought to be the first time. Beyond the immediate problem related to Olmec culture, the investigations have greater significance.

The limited example of the derivation of two inferred sequences of Olmec objects argues well for the wide application of the methodology I have described. It should be possible to break down into their constituent elements or traits any relatively homogeneous group of objects. These could be primarily utilitarian or primarily artistic; a system of writing or a set of paintings would lend themselves equally well to such treatment. By following the Guttman procedure it could be determined which of these elements are scalable.

Traits so isolated may be explained by a single underlying causal factor. The nature of this factor can be inferred from the configuration of the traits; the question being whether differences in the scalable traits are of degree or of kind.

If there are differences of degree the inference might be that evolutionary sequence is present. To determine which end of an evolutionary sequence falls later in time, the principle of functional prerequisiteness can be employed. At the same time the possibility of a degenerative or disintegrative process being responsible for scaling must never be ignored.

If differences of kind are obscure this may mean that more than one object category is present (as with Olmec votive axes). It might be inferred further that different artists or even different cultures created the products under scrutiny.

The field of archaeology is beset by puzzles requiring for their solution the classification and ordering of sets of objects. The Guttman scale is a powerful tool for this task. It can test dozens of traits at the same time efficiently and quickly. The mental gymnastics to achieve the same results without using the scale technique would require an exceptional mind and great expenditure of effort and time. In much the same way the use of statistics saves time and effort in experimental science because it permits more than one variable to be tested in a single experiment.

Problems of classification and ordering are not unique to archaeology. They occur throughout science. Thus the application of Guttman scaling seems limitless. Developmental natural sequences treated in such fields as biology, physics, geology, and astronomy could be clarified and refined by the Guttman technique. In the field of culture history the process of micro-evolution may be detected whether the focus be an invention, an idea, or an art style.

Application of the Guttman scale in the present case has given us two solid sequences for Olmec art. The sequences are not impressionistic. Their bases rest on mathematics rather than subjectivity. In his original formulation, Guttman (1941) presented step-by-step the mathematical foundations which underlie scaling.

The ordering of the Olmec Colossal Heads and votive axes is grounded in several internal consistencies revealed by scaling. To account for these consistencies I have inferred a constant and regular change over time. For the Colossal Heads this change involves the evolution of facial expression from serenity to a smiling countenance to a lack of animation. In proportion to height the heads become steadily wider and deeper. The eyes lose their well-defined iris.

Within the votive axe sequence the hand becomes more elaborate. This development is analogous to the stages in which an individual artist might sketch a hand: first a blocking out, then a distinguishing of the fingers, and finally the shaping of the hand with the thumb. For the votive axes which depict adult beings, the fangs become steadily more complex. Straight fangs are followed by curved ones, which, in turn, lead to double fangs. At the same time, headbands give way to plaques above the eyes.

I consider these constructions solid enough to allow for further inferences. Olmec style could well have evolved in the manner that has been deduced from scaling. This comes to bear on several aspects of the Olmec problem: the geographical origins of Olmec art, the role of La Venta in the history of the Olmecs and the influences of Olmec art on that of later cultures. In the following chapter these topics will be considered in detail.

5

The Olmec Problem
Reconsidered

OF WHAT UTILITY in illuminating the Olmec problem is our ordering of Olmec Colossal Heads and votive axes? What can the Guttman scalograms tell us about the Olmec that is not already known? I think that the scalograms demonstrated in the previous chapter serve a significant role in a systematic attack on the Olmec problem. Correlated with theories of the growth of civilization, ecological considerations, and evidence from archaeological investigations, the Guttman scalograms constitute one more building block in the body of knowledge about the Olmec.

The sequence for votive axes gives a good idea of how all Olmec art might have evolved. For it and for the Colossal Head sequence the cause of variation in scaled traits is held to be evolution over time; no other causal factors suggest themselves. I do not believe that regional variation, for example, could express itself in this way; it would lack the "flow" of the objects arranged in sequence.

The votive axe sequence shows much greater internal differences than does that for the Colossal Heads. It appears, therefore, that the evolution of the votive axes involved considerably more time: i.e., a macro-evolution as opposed to a micro-evolution. The evolutionary sequence for axes, because it presumably took place over a much greater time span, seems much more important for an understanding of the evolution of Olmec art than that of the Colossal Heads.

The Colossal Heads in Archaeological Context

As has been mentioned, the sequence of Colossal Heads, when considered in the light of Coe's findings at San Lorenzo, might indicate shifts of political power in the Olmec heartland from San Lorenzo to La Venta to Tres Zapotes. In this connection, it should be recalled that both San Lorenzo and La Venta apparently were abandoned after their Olmec occupation. At San Lorenzo monuments were ritually buried; at La Venta they were left in place. In contrast, after the Olmec occupation at Tres Zapotes life continued.

How did Olmec style cease to be at Tres Zapotes? Was the ending sudden or gradual? What social forces were behind the termination of Olmec style? If a peasant revolt took place, hierarchic art should disappear literally overnight. If an invasion took place, a new hierarchic art should appear. If the monuments were destroyed in later times as part of a campaign to rewrite history or revolutionize religion, this, too, could be detected archaeologically.

Up to the present, archaeological work carried out at Tres Zapotes has been aimed more at recovering monuments than at

answering such questions as we pose. Because of this, the monuments at Tres Zapotes lack sound archaeological contexts.
They must speak to us in almost total isolation.

The two Colossal Heads constitute in themselves half of
the Olmec monuments known from Tres Zapotes. The other
two are Stela C and Monument C. Stela C carries on one dam-
aged face a bar-and-dot date (Fig. 14) of 31 B.C. in the GMT
correlation and on the other a highly stylized jaguar mask
(Fig. 15). Monument C (Fig. 2), a badly broken stone box,
carries a mask at top center so stylized that there is no certainty
of its being feline. (Two claws much like those on the Aztec
sculpture of the earth deity Coatlicue are below on either side
of the mask.) From the mask flows a complex pattern of volutes
among which floating warriors brandish clubs as on Stela 2
from La Venta (Fig. 7).

Jiménez Moreno (1959) suggests that the inscription on
Stela C constitutes an Olmec testament. A people invading from
the Maya region are held responsible for the bar-and-dot Long
Count date. Olmec culture ends in the heartland because of the
expansive force of Maya culture.

Opposed to Jiménez's admittedly unorthodox opinion is
Coe's idea of a largely independent evolution of Olmec style
leading to something different. Certainly, the diverging views
of Jiménez and Coe form a common plea for additional work —
problem-oriented excavations — at Tres Zapotes.

Coe (1965a: 773) focuses on Monument C — much as
Jiménez fixes upon Stela C as embodying his thesis — as a work
intermediate between the earlier Olmec and the later Izapa
style. The style takes its name from the Chiapas Pacific slope
site visited by Stirling in 1941 and 1945. According to Coe,
before diffusing to Izapa, it first grew out of the Olmec tradition
at Tres Zapotes. In turn Izapa style led to the Classic Maya
style. Izapa differs from Olmec style in being anecdotal and
cluttered, and in depicting feather headdresses while ignoring
feline motifs.

Olmec Influence on Maya Art

In my own view, the influence of Olmec art on the Maya in many instances could have been more direct than through an intermediate style. Indeed, the sequence of Olmec votive axes seems to express an evolution leading almost up to the Maya style. Let us consider a specific instance.

J. Eric Thompson (1954: 46-47) characterizes the large stucco masks flanking the staircase on Pyramid E-VII sub at Uaxactún, Petén, Guatemala, as "distinctly Rococo." Because the pyramid dates from the Formative or Preclassic period, its art style seems incongruent to Thompson, "although, as far as we know, this is an incipient, not a decadent art." In describing the masks, he says:

The curled tusks at the corners of the mouths, the eyebrows with accentuated shagginess, the flat snouts, and the peculiar half-tongue, half-incisor pendent from the upper lip leave little doubt that the jaguar god is here displayed.

In view of the evolutionary sequence shown for Olmec votive axes, the curled tusks and shaggy eyebrows would leave little doubt that the E-VII sub masks are not the products of an incipient art at all. Curled fangs and shaggy eye plaques are characteristic of Late Olmec art. The masks evolve directly out of the Late Olmec style.

Other Maya forms are reminiscent of Olmec prototypes. Figures within niches, for example, as on stelae from Piedras Negras, Petén, Guatemala, could well have evolved from the niche figurines on Olmec tabletop altars. With complete data, a satisfactory sequence might be worked out using Guttman scaling. Subjectively, I see a sequence beginning with Altar 6 at La Venta (Fig. 35) in which a cubistic figure sits cross-legged with his back against the solid altar block. This is followed by Altar 2 at La Venta (Fig. 18) with a shallow carving away following the shoulders. A deeper and more rounded niche is shown by Altar 4 (Fig. 8) and Altar 5 (Fig. 16) at La Venta. With Altar 3 (Fig. 36) the niche has expanded to the extent that its upper part has blended with the ledge of the tabletop on

Fig. 35. Altar 6, La Venta

the altar, thereby losing its roundness and becoming rectangular. Because of this, Altar 3 at La Venta seems closest to those at Piedras Negras.

If Maya figures-in-niches indeed evolved from Olmec prototypes, the form might have followed the same function in both Maya and Olmec culture. Although ignorant of the functions of figures in niches among the Olmec, we can seize upon a hypothesis that has been formed about the better-known Maya examples. Perhaps this hypothesis might hold true for Olmec monuments. While readily acknowledging that building one hypothesis upon another weakens my formulation, I should like us to consider some recent ideas about Maya monuments. By doing so, we gain insight into the possible function of certain of the Olmec monoliths.

Fig. 36. Altar 3, La Venta

Tatiana Proskouriakoff (1960) holds that the monuments at Piedras Negras fall into distinct series. Their dates, physical grouping, and the repetition of glyphs and motifs all point to the sculpture having "the qualities one might expect of a historical narrative" (p. 455). David Kelley's (1962) investigations of glyphs at Quiriguá, Guatemala, reveal similar sequences. Specifically, each series of monuments supposedly depicts a standard set of events in the life of a particular ruler: his birthday or confirmation day, the inaugural of his rule, his death, and other milestones. Maya niched figures, which at Piedras Negras occur in such series, are credited by Proskouriakoff with indicating an inauguration. The personage, dressed in ceremonial garb, is seated in a niche below which is a ladder with footprints — Proskouriakoff's "ascension motif" — and above which is a "sky band."

Morley (1946: Plate 66) shows four such sculptures from Piedras Negras. In comparing the La Venta examples with these, general resemblances can be noted, such as the attitude of the figure and the ceremonial garb of headdress and collar. More specifically, Altar 4, La Venta (Fig. 8), shows an abstract feline head which may be the homologue of the *moan* bird head centered above the niche in the Maya examples. Olmec niched monuments lack the ascension motif, but a Saint Andrew's cross is set between the fangs of the Altar 4 feline. This motif, flanked by two vertical elements, is characteristic of the Maya sky or planetary band. Of more importance in making a case for this particular Olmec-Maya connection is the appearance of two prisoners (or slaves or diffident subjects) at the feet of personages centered on many of the stones that form the Maya series. Altar 4 at La Venta, which shows bound prisoners at either end, could well be a prototype for the Maya monuments.

Not all the niched Olmec figures suggest ascension or inauguration. Those showing infants in the outstretched arms of a seated figure most likely correspond to those members of a Maya series which show the birthday or confirmation day of a ruler. Some specialists read infant sacrifice into the Olmec monuments, and it is known that the Aztecs sacrificed babies to the rain god, Tlaloc, in times of drought. Yet the Olmec "babes in arms" monuments and their smaller counterparts (Fig. 28) portray no sacrificial scenes. Furthermore, sufficient rainfall would not seem to have been a problem in the Olmec heartland; only the control of rainfall, its distribution in time, possibly could have concerned the inhabitants of the rain forests of Tabasco and southern Veracruz.

As has been suggested, the death of an Olmec ruler could have been commemorated in the carving of a Colossal Head.

Does the physical grouping of Olmec monuments obey the same rules as that of the Maya? Comparative data for the solution of the problem are lacking. Only from La Venta do we have such information. At San Lorenzo, the Colossal Heads and other monuments were uprooted in ancient times and deposited elsewhere.

Perhaps three of the four Colossal Heads' being set in a row at La Venta could be meaningful. Whereas at Piedras Negras the monuments relating to the life of one individual usually are grouped in a row in front of a temple pyramid, it is possible that at La Venta similar series were strung out behind the Colossal Heads parallel to the central axis of the site (Fig. 17).

All this is conjecture. The evolutionary series obtained for the Colossal Heads, the possibility of a similar series for Olmec altars combined with Proskouriakoff's thesis on the function of Maya monuments have led me to set down these speculations in the hope that they will lead to rewarding paths of inquiry.

Olmec Influence on Classic Veracruz Art

Olmec art apparently not only influenced the Maya style which developed to the southeast of the heartland, but that of the Classic period of central Veracruz to the north. Olmec art is linked to Classic Veracruz and Maya art through what Covarrubias (1957: 166-67) has called a "transitional style," the hallmark of which is the volute. The volute or scroll meander becomes all-pervasive in the Classic Veracruz or Tajín style usually attributed to the Totonacs.

We have observed the volute on the late Olmec or transitional sculptures of Monument C, Tres Zapotes (Fig. 2) and on the Chalcatzingo reliefs (Fig. 10). It is to them that we must look for the origin of the meander of the art of the Mesoamerican Classic period.

Proskouriakoff (1953: 389), in a study of scroll patterns, ignores their possible origin, but she notes:

Although the Maya and the Classic Veracruz styles are very different and show little evidence of direct contact with one another, both have a strong predilection for the form known as the scroll. Moreover, in both the form is drawn with rhythmic curvatures, a manner which is characteristic of art styles of the Classic period over most of Middle America.

Chalcatzingo volutes are less intricate than those of Monument C from Tres Zapotes; both are more simple than those of Tajín yokes or Maya marble vessels from the Ulúa region of Honduras. Thus, the late Olmec or transitional style seemingly can be tied into the artistic traditions that followed it. Since a developmental sequence probably exists within Mesoamerica, the inspiration for the complex patterns of the Classic (A.D. 300-900) from China during Late Chou times (700-200 B.C.) suggested by Ekholm (1964: 498-99) seem rather tenuous.

Significance of the Votive Axe Sequence

It is to China as well that several champions of trans-Pacific diffusion tentatively look as a source for the feline motif. Ekholm (1964: 503-4) considers this a "likely prospect" that "should be studied in detail"; he continues:

It is of special interest because the Olmec culture appears at the present stage of knowledge to be the earliest of the high cultures of Mesoamerica and presents some extraordinarily sophisticated features for which no previous developmental sequence has yet been found. In a general way the

Olmec culture would seem to have possible relationships to early bronze-age China, specifically, the cultures of the Shang dynasty dating from the sixteenth century B.C. to 1027 B.C. Not many trait resemblances are found, but one must look with suspicion at the great emphasis on the tiger motif in both Shang and Olmec art . . . .

The lacking developmental sequence lamented by Ekholm has now been found. The technique of Guttman scaling has revealed the chart in Fig. 34. It shows, in one form, the evolution of the Olmec style. Most likely, the earlier feline motifs were inspired by jaguars, pumas, and other cats of the immediate physical environment. From simple designs evolved the more complex configurations of Olmec art at the height of its development.

Most of the monoliths of the Olmec heartland were created toward the end of the development attested by the scalograms. Because the Olmec art style appears fullblown in the Tabasco-southern Veracruz region many authorities feel it did not evolve there.

The question of Olmec origins is one of the major problems in Mesoamerican archaeology today. No general agreement exists on the point of origin. The question has more than historical interest; a theoretical problem is involved as well. Mesoamerican archaeologists who have interested themselves in the ecological problem of the environmental conditions necessary to allow for the earliest beginnings of civilization are divided into a highland school and a lowland school.

Michael Coe (1963: 32), who champions the lowlands, stresses that the Gulf Coast of southern Veracruz with rich alluvial soils and a growing season much longer than that of the highlands is ". . . the place of origin of the Mesoamerican Formative, where village-farming became a way of life for the first time."

William Sanders (1963: 973), exponent of the highland school, gives an important role in the formation of civilization to highland hydraulic agriculture as a cultural reply to "the

type of challenge offered by arid regions in which large coop-
erative groups are necessary for effective manipulation of the
environment."

Because many ramifications of culture theory are involved
in accepting either posture, emotions run high in the demi-
world of Mesoamerican archaeology when the differing views
are aired. Personally, I have no emotional stake in this question
at the moment. Statistical tests, the Guttman included, are un-
emotional. The Guttman scalogram of the characteristics of
Olmec votive axes points to a highland origin for Olmec style
and culture.

One way to tackle the problem of the origin of Olmec style
would be to delimit the area of provenience for the axes earliest
in the sequence. Two objections to this procedure become immediately apparent, however. In the first place, the provenience data do not seem reliable. In the second, Olmec votive
axes constitute *art mobilier;* they are light enough to have been
carried far and wide. Thus, where they were found may tell
little about where they were created. Axe G in Fig. 34 was discovered by Stirling in a La Venta tomb. Stylistically it belongs
to those axes latest in the inferred sequence. José Luís Franco
assures me that what I have called the Ekholm axe (Fig. 34),
without doubt comes from Yucuquimi in the Mixteca Alta of
Oaxaca. It belongs to axes earliest in the sequence. This would
make a case for Olmec stylistic origins in the highlands of western Oaxaca and a stylistic maturation in the Gulf Coast lowlands, were it not for the axes being easily transportable.

Certainly we would have a much stronger case if massive
monolithic sculptures sharing the traits of the earliest axes
were found in the highlands of Oaxaca. At least one such monolith exists; this is the reason for concluding that the Olmec style
first flowered in the Mixteca Alta.

In arriving at this conclusion, however, it is best to work
backward from the better known to the less known. I have
mentioned that the axes regarded as latest in the series show

individual traits which are shared by the monolithic sculpture of the La Venta site. Conversely, no large sculpture in the La Venta or Olmec heartland region shows traits in common with the axes lowest on the scale. Because of this I hold that the artistic developments of the Tabasco-southern Veracruz region come relatively late in the Olmec tradition.

The monolithic sculptre of La Venta, San Lorenzo, and Tres Zapotes is too large to have been transported very far. Heizer and Williams (1960) believe that volcanic rock from the western flanks of the Tuxtla mountains was used at Tres Zapotes and San Lorenzo while La Unión volcano, south of Villahermosa, could be the source for the La Venta lithic material. Presumably it was shipped into the sites on rafts and sculptured there, although no work areas have been found or looked for (Heizer 1962: 315). Their massiveness makes Olmec monoliths the antithesis of *art mobilier*.

Just as the delightful nudes on Attic red-figured vessels are part of the same artistic movement as the pediment sculpture of Greece in mid-fifth century B.C., so do the motifs of Olmec *art mobilier* relate to monolithic sculpture. Olmec votive axes were not created in a cultural vacuum. They are part of an all-embracing stylistic development. It is for this reason that the chronology of the Olmec heartland sites worked out by radiocarbon dating gives us some idea of the temporal situation of the votive axes.

The upper row of Fig. 34 shows axes with serrated eye-plaques and curved fangs. They were created at the same time as monuments from La Venta with the same features. The La Venta sarcophagus (Fig. 15), Monument 15 (Fig. 15), and Altar 1 (Fig. 31) all show these stylistic manifestations. In all likelihood the La Venta monuments were fashioned during the time span 800-400 B.C., placing them within the Middle Preclassic. The terminal Lower Preclassic from 1200 to 850 B.C., immediately preceding La Venta, is the time span for San Lorenzo. An example of monolithic sculpture from this San

Lorenzo period is the anthropomorphic jaguar, Monument 10, in Fig. 20. By comparing it with the votive axes in Fig. 34, it becomes obvious that Monument 10 shares traits with those in the middle of the sequence — in rows 2 and 3 — because of its banded headdress and only slightly curving fangs. This causes me to believe that the stylistic mannerisms of the pieces in rows 2 and 3 belong to the latter half of the Lower Preclassic. By default, the remaining row might belong to the earlier half of the Lower Preclassic (1600-1200 B.C.).

No monolithic sculpture yet found in the Gulf Coast heartland is comparable stylistically to the axes of the lowest row in Fig. 34 which we equate with the first half of the Lower Preclassic. Perhaps, then, we should look away from the tropical heartland and up to the temperate highlands. Were it possible to relate large Olmec sculpture to the axes lowermost in the series, as we have done with the other rows, an excellence case would be made for the place of origin for Olmec style.

San Martín Huamelulpan

Within the Mixteca Alta of the State of Oaxaca — at latitude 17 degrees, 24 minutes north and 97 degrees longitude — nestles San Martín Huamelulpan. Though close to the equator, its 7,011 feet elevation makes for cool winters and moderate summers. A massive hill towers behind the town, its terraced silhouette indicating that in Precolumbian times it was covered by a city. Little work has been done thus far on the site, and, consequently, little is known about it.

None of the Huamelulpan inhabitants remembers exactly on what date some twenty or thirty years ago a cigar-shaped sculpture was rolled from the site above the town. It was set up at the entrance of what was then the San Martín school building and is now the mayor's office. Almost a meter high, it gazes on all who climb the steps to enter the municipal headquarters. The gaze is unabashedly Olmec (Fig. 37).

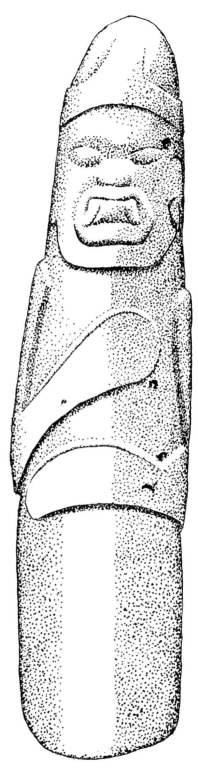

Fig. 37. Monolith, Huamelulpan, Mixteca Alta

The San Martín Huamelulpan monolith gives the appearance of an Olmec votive axe enlarged balloon-like. Its features are those of axes belonging to the lowest row in our series: axes inferred to be the earliest. Its fangs, hands one above the other, and its undivided head place it within the series on the right side in Fig. 34. Thus it is an adult jaguar-human with fangs rather than an infant like the axes to the left with gums and V-slit in the center of the head. More significant are the traits which would place the Huamelulpan monolith vertically in the scale: hand-type, fangs, and treatment above the eye. The hand-type is blocky without fingers; fangs are slightly curved; treatment above the eye is a band. Each one of these features places the monolithic sculpture with the axes lowest in the series.

The Huamelulpan site is almost untouched archaeologically. Alfonso Caso and Lorenzo Gamio dug there during two weeks in 1961, but published no report. A monolithic stairway and adjoining platform adorned with calendaric glyphs of Monte Albán II style were uncovered. The ceramics gathered from the fill of the platform belong to Monte Albán I types, perhaps indicating a time lag between ceramics and sculptural style (Paddock 1966: 126). The structure would have been built within the Upper Preclassic at least a millennium after the era that we infer for the creation of the Huamelulpan Olmec monolith. Because only a few square meters have been sampled archaeologically out of several square kilometers, the discrepancy is not surprising. All phases of the long Preclassic development might well be represented at Huamelulpan. Illegal excavations in the region seemingly have produced Olmec ceramics: Mexico City dealers in antiquities have been selling such pieces which purportedly come from northwestern Oaxaca.

Geographically, San Martín Huamelulpan is situated at the end of a corridor that leads right into the Olmec heartland. The area around Huamelulpan is drained to the northeast by the Santo Domingo River which flows into the Papaloapan. The Papaloapan discharges into the Gulf of Mexico slightly north of

Tres Zapotes (Fig. 1). Because of this canyon passageway, a close cultural connection between the Mixteca Alta and the southern Veracruz-northern Tabasco region is certainly feasible.

Guerrero

Another river corridor passes from the Huamelulpan region across the State of Guerrero. The Mixteco River flows northward to the northwest corner of Oaxaca, then curves to the west to join the Balsas which cuts across the State of Guerrero to empty into the Pacific. According to Covarrubias (1957: 76), Olmec art "may well have had its origins . . . in the valleys of the Pacific slopes of Oaxaca and Guerrero, where its most archaic forms appear." Covarrubias's impressionistic, subjective view as to what constitutes the archaic forms of Olmec art coincides with my ordering of Olmec votive axes by Guttman scaling. The presence of these archaic forms in the Balsas drainage strengthens the case for the San Martín Huamelulpan area as the center of the production of the earliest Olmec art.

Monte Alban

Jiménez Moreno (1959: 1030) speaks of La Venta and Monte Albán during the Middle Preclassic as the highest evolved Mesoamerican centers, as maintaining contact, and as forming a "civilizing axis." However, as Jiménez adds, at this time the LaVenta area lacked the system of calendaric glyphs characteristic of Monte Albán I. It would appear that had the two centers had close and constant ties, the glyphic system found at Monte Albán during Period I would have been manifest on the stone monuments at La Venta. Such is not the case. The only obvious example of glyphic notation appears on Monument 13 at the Tabasco site (Fig. 33). The glyphs are somewhat reminiscent of those on the Monte Albán "danzantes" because of their paucity and simplicity (Fig. 38). At La Venta,

Fig. 38. Danzante, Monte Albán, Oaxaca

however, nothing compares with the complex columns of glyphs and bar-and-dot numerals of the stelae from Period I of Monte Albán.

My hypothesis is that the similarities and differences are the result of the two sites sharing a common cultural heritage. Reflecting this, the relatively undifferentiated style of the Huamelulpan monolith could have given rise to the "danzantes" in the Valley of Oaxaca. Within the highlands of Oaxaca its evolution could have shown a different pattern than that demonstrated by Guttman scaling to account for the Olmec heartland style.

Interestingly enough, Caso (1965: 855) mentions the Huamelulpan sculpture in a discussion of the "danzantes," although without attempting to diagnose its relationship. Thick, downturned lips which bare the teeth, almond eyes, and short, wide noses are shared by "danzantes" and the Huamelulpan image. Furthermore, in the "danzante" type considered oldest by Caso (1965: 851) "fingers are sometimes not apparent." The style of the Huamelulpan monolith could be the prototype for both Olmec heartland and Oaxaca Valley Middle Preclassic sculpture. Both could have grown out of a style which emerged at a geographically intermediate locus: the Mixteca Alta of Oaxaca.

Some evolution undoubtedly took place within the Mixteca Alta itself. A sculpture found by Sigvald Linné in a cave southeast of Diquiyú — itself north of Huamelulpan near Tezoatlan — shows traits of axes intermediate in our sequence except that its arms are crossed over the chest. Fingers are rudimentary and the headband is like those of axes B and Q in Fig. 34. The wide nose and thick, downturned lips are also shared with the votive axes. At its discovery, the almost meter-high idol was still in active service: its head garlanded and at its feet offerings of chickens, eggs, and fifteen centavos (Martí 1965 abc).

Connections with Peru

Not only do the rivers that arise in the area around Huamelulpan flow northeast to the Olmec heartland and on to the west through Guerrero, but they flow to the south as well. The Verde River drains the area south of Huamelulpan and discharges in the Pacific Ocean as does the Balsas farther north. Easy access to the Pacific coast might have characterized the area where Olmec style originated. Olmec style is strikingly similar to a contemporary style with easy access to the American Pacific: the style of the Chavín of Peru. Like Olmec art, Chavín manifests a preoccupation with feline motifs.

Connections between the two styles are by no means superficial. Of the cultures that gave rise to them, Coe (1963a: 34) believes that "Olmec culture is the full equivalent both in temporal and in typological sense, of Chavín in Peru, with which it was probably connected through long-range diffusion." The Peruvian coastal manifestation of the Chavín style is called Cupisnique and it shares with the Olmec Tlatilco culture of the Valley of Mexico: "stirrup-spout jars, bottles, zoned dentate rocker-stamping, color-zoning, animal effigies, split-face dualism, and the jaguar or were-jaguar as a cult motif" (Coe 1963b: 102).

David B. Smith considers the incised figures on stone slabs at Cerro Sechín, Casma Valley, Peru, to be influenced by the Olmec style. He and Coe independently arrived at the impression that some of the pottery from Kotosh in the central highlands of Peru show Olmec influence. Smith (quoted in Kidder 1964: 460) says:

We see the real possibility that Olmec may have directly or indirectly influenced the northern coast of Peru at a time prior to the full development of Classic Chavín art as known at Chavín de Huantar . . . and at such places as Cerro Blanco in the Nepeña Valley and at Moxeke in Casma Valley. At any rate, after a thousand years of settled agriculture something sets off a florescence of art and the first indications that the communities of a region are united in common economic, religious, artistic and architectural endeavors.

Kidder (1964: 461, Fig. 6) illustrates an example of what Smith is speaking of: a turquoise head from the northern coast of Peru. It appears to me to be purest Olmec style.

Perhaps a little more tenuous is the "Olmec design" on a vessel from Kotosh, in the central Peruvian highlands. The design is an ear of maize highly stylized in the Olmec manner. It appears on a pre-Chavín bottle. From this Coe (1962) makes a case for Olmec culture beginning before Chavín, but not without considerable objections from Peruvian specialist Edward Lanning (1963). Though agreeing with Coe, I would at least grant to Lanning that the traffic was two way. The stone slabs from Placeres de Oro, Guerrero, depicted by Covarrubias (1957: 113) in noting their "Chavín style," seem proof enough.

Coe (1963b: 104) explains the stylistic similarities of Olmec and Chavín:

Coincident with the ascent of Olmec, a long-range, maritime, trading network had been established between the Pacific coasts of Mesoamerica and Ecuador. This route, or an extension of it, could have been utilized by Olmec or Olmecoid missionaries and traders to reach Peru, perhaps as early as 1000 B.C. . . . . The Mesoamericans would have introduced, along with a Tlatilco-like ceramic complex, the Olmec art style and Olmec religion, centering on the worship of a large spotted cat with snarling mouth, a feline which could only be a jaguar. The curvilinear, "realistic," and basically sculptural art style merged with the native Peruvian canon based on fabric structure to produce the art of Chavín . . . .

A sculpture found by Edwin Ferdon (1953) on the Pacific coast of Mexico at Tonalá, Chiapas, points to an early Olmec penetration to the Tehuantepec littoral. Although smaller and less elaborate than the Huamelulpan monolith, it shares some of the same early Olmec features: straight fangs and simple treatment above the eyes. The Tehuantepec shore well could have been a takeoff point for cultural influences from Mesoamerica to the South American coast early in history.

From the similarities of Olmec and Chavín art styles we cannot necessarily infer migrations of large groups of people, however. Nor can we infer the sharing of an identical religion in Mesoamerica and the Andean area. The similarities in Olmec and Chavín art are more likely reflections of a diffusion of similar ideologies — certain basic ideas about the nature of the universe — within the two areas. For ideas to diffuse, migrations of peoples are unnecessary. As we shall mention, these early pan-American ideologies could have diffused along with knowledge of agriculture.

However this might have been, the ideologies would have been strongly held and would have persisted in time. The concept of the anthropomorphised feline, fundamental to Olmec thought, is also strongly expressed in Chavín art. The belief in a cat ancestor was likely shared by both cultures. Rafael Larco Hoyle has called my attention to Mochica pottery vessels portraying felines and humanized felines copulating with human females. Although Mochica comes after Chavín, the erotic Mochica ceramic art might indicate the persistence of certain ideas from the earlier period. Larco's examples reminded me of the Olmec Stone pieces from the Río Chiquito region which depict the same event (Figs. 19, 22). In their composition, however, the Mochica pieces seem more like the figures of Relief IV discovered at Chalcatzingo, Morelos, in the summer of 1964. These late Olmec works picture two humans lying face up, each being "attacked" by a snarling, clawing cat (Gay 1966: 60).

A sharing of ideologies reflected in similarities of Olmec and Chavín style may have significant implications for the study of culture growth. Only in Mesoamerica and in the Andean area did civilization develop in the New World. Only where Olmec and Chavín art appears in the millennium before Christ do complex societies arise in the millennium after. Is there a connection between the styles and the later development? Gordon Willey (1962: 9-10) thinks so. He makes a telling point in holding that within these styles are

the symbols for the religious ideologies of the early farming societies of Mesoamerica and Peru . . . that in these ideologies these early societies had developed a mechanism of intercommunication, a way of knitting together the smaller parts of the social universe of their day into a more unified whole than it had heretofore been or would otherwise be . . . . The sharing of common ideologies led to the threshold of civilization by enlarging the effective social field. By this enlargement more individuals, more social segments, more local societies combined and coordinated their energies and efforts than at any time before.

Early Plant Domestication

The recent pioneering work by MacNeish (1964) on plant domestication shows that many New World foods — including the essential staple maize — were developed somewhere in the Mexican highlands south of Mexico City and north of Chiapas. San Martín Huamelulpan, where Olmec style might have originated, lies midway in this zone.

Perhaps Huamelulpan's being within the area of Mesoamerica where the discovery of maize agriculture took place is no mere coincidence. The domestication of plants might be causally connected with the emergence of a sophisticated art style.

Of course, the causal relations are intricate between the invention of agriculture and the rise of civilization with its great art styles. To date they have proved too complex to have been unraveled by social scientists. Correlations involving feedback must have obtained between technological advances, population increase, growth of cities, crystallization of social strata, flowering of great art styles, enlargement of knowledge, and developments in religion.

The evolution of Olmec art would presumably correlate with the evolution in Olmec religion, for example. The religion, in turn, would support new ideas such as the accumulation of social surpluses and the divine right of some individuals to more power and privilege than others. In this way, Olmec religion, of which Olmec art is an expression, might be seen as emerging along with the new way of life made possible by agriculture. The religion would furnish the farmer with the *raison d'être* behind parting with a portion of his produce.

As agriculture diffused, religion diffused along with it. Perhaps this is the most likely explanation for the presence in the Andean area of the Chavín art style. It is known that food plants such as maize and beans were introduced from Mesoamerica into Precolumbian Peru. Agricultural techniques, perhaps involving irrigation, could have gone along. The religious basis for this new economic and social order would not have been far behind.

A key feature of the new social order is professionalism. It is my opinion that the Huamelulpan monument may be one of the first sculptures produced in Mesoamerica by a full-time artisan. Certainly the Huamelulpan sculpture had antecedents; it could hardly have appeared out of nothing. But these antecedents were non-professional. The crude sculpture on boulders of the Pacific slope (Miles 1965) that could have preceded it bespeaks neither professionalism nor the Olmec style. It is only from the Huamelulpan sculpture that the La Venta style can be shown to evolve directly. It is only from the Huamelulpan sculpture that we can infer the beginnings of professionalism.

With the rise of the first full-time specialists in the arts, other specialists are surely present. The patrons of the artists were likely full-time priest rulers or chieftains. These individuals were persuasive enough to bring about the accumulation of social surpluses. Despite claims to the contrary, theirs must truly have been the earliest profession. Hence, with the emergence of what we infer to be the art of professionals, begins in Mesoamerica a process — with perhaps far-reaching effects in Peru — which led to the complex division of labor characteristic of civilization. Thus, for the New World both agriculture and what we might call a proto-civilization evolved in the same region. This seems not to have happened in the Old World.

Caso's Mesopotamian Parallel

For the Near East, Braidwood (1960) has demonstrated the earliest domestication of wheat and barley on the upland flanks of the Fertile Crescent to the north and east of the Tigris-Euphrates Valley. Only after village agriculture was well under way in the upland area did the practice of agriculture descend to the desert plains. For this to come about, irrigation had to be discovered. Only by irrigation techniques could the desert of the Tigris-Euphrates floodplain be cultivated. It is likely that natural flooding, characteristic of the delta area, served to inspire the development of irrigation.

In contrast to civilizations of the Near East, Mesoamerican civilization did not flourish in deserts. Nevertheless, Alfonso Caso (1965) looks to Mesopotamia for parallels with which to account for the flowering of early civilization in Mesoamerica. Caso characterizes the predominating agricultural system of the Mexican tropical lowlands as wasteful; the slash-and-burn method requires enormous expenditures of human energy and the allocation of vast tracts of fallow land. The latter feature dictates semipermanent or shifting settlements. Unpromising for the growth of civilization, this agricultural system contrasts markedly with that of the Olmec heartland. In the heartland area, according to Caso, a more efficient system of land use could have been followed: floodplain irrigation. For this reason Caso names the area the "Mesoamerican Mesopotamia."

With irrigation agriculture permanent settlements were possible. During the rainy season the rivers swell to overflow their banks in the plain of southern Veracruz and northern Tabasco. They deposit regenerative silt over the fields along watercourses; consequently new fields do not have to be cleared of jungle growth. Caso notes that La Venta, Tres Zapotes, and the Río Chiquito complex — Olmec sites *par excellence* — are all located on the banks of rivers astride floodplains with deep rich soil.

Caso's ideas place him in opposition to Heizer (1962) and others who assume that slash-and-burn farming techniques alone gave economic support to La Venta culture. Before Caso's views can be considered more than conjecture, much research must be done on the questions they raise. Ancient floodplain irrigation would be difficult to prove archaeologically in an alluvial region unless stone dams or stone-lined canals had been constructed. (Stone conduits do occur at San Lorenzo, but their function is not yet demonstrated.) As supporting evidence, documents from the area in the sixteenth century could prove illuminating, especially if about litigation involving riparian rights. Ethnographic descriptions of floodplain irrigation carried on by peoples of low technology in tropical environments would also be of great utility in approaching the problem.

Whatever occurred in the Olmec heartland area of southern Veracruz and northern Tabasco at the time when Olmec art reached its culmination, it would not alter our basic arguments that the Olmec style had its origin in the highland area of the Mixteca Alta.

Conclusions and Speculations

At the close of Chapter 1 the Olmec problem was broken down into subdivisions. For one of these — the question of the ultimate origin of the Olmec style — four possibilities were listed: 1) early bronze-age China, proposed by Gordon Ekholm; 2) the Olmec heartland of coastal southern Veracruz and northern Tabasco, favored by Caso and Coe; 3) Piña Chan's highland origin centering on the State of Morelos; and 4) Covarrubias's highland Pacific slope of Oaxaca and Guerrero. The solution that we have proposed most nearly coincides with Covarrubias's location of the Pacific slope, and is not unlike Piña's.

A combination of our objective statistical methodology with direct reasoning has produced an alternative for Olmec origins, already proposed by Covarrubias on subjective grounds. The style of Olmec pieces from Guerrero and Oaxaca seemed to Covarrubias more archaic than that of Olmec artifacts from elsewhere.

In retrospect, the area indicated seems ideally situated for the spread of Olmec style and culture. It is close to Morelos; river pathways connect it with the Gulf coast heartland region, central Guerrero, and the Oaxaca Pacific coast. The Pacific coast region would have served for active intercourse with the partly contemporary Chavín culture of Peru.

Although we are thus able to give an answer to the heretofore unsolved problem of Olmec origins, the solution to other enigmas posed by the Olmecs must be more speculative. Chronology remains unsolved. The earliest radiocarbon date for a major site of the Olmec heartland so far is that obtained by Michael Coe for San Lorenzo of *c.* 1200 B.C. This is 400 years earlier than the beginnings of La Venta indicated by radiocarbon dating. If this is an essentially correct interpretation of the radiocarbon analyses, the beginnings of Olmec style at Huamelulpan, Oaxaca, go back into the Lower Preclassic, perhaps as early as 1600 B.C. Frankly, this is highly speculative. All that we claim to have shown is that the Huamelulpan monolith is older than other Olmec sculpture, but we can only guess at how much. Several centuries of evolution seemingly were required to bridge the gap between the simplicity of Huamelulpan art and the relative complexity of that on the Gulf Coast.

As for the end of the Olmec style, the view could be held that in merging with the Classic styles it did not die at all. The Olmec style seems to have persisted despite radical social changes implied by the enigmatic burying of Olmec monuments at San Lorenzo, their abandonment at La Venta, and their seemingly purposeful destruction at what might have been the last Olmec political center, Tres Zapotes.

Stela C at Tres Zapotes appears to be a key monument in understanding the demise of the Olmecs. Its bar-and-dot date has been interpreted as 31 B.C., using the Goodman-Martínez-Thompson correlation under the assumption that the Maya calendaric system and the one at Tres Zapotes used the same starting point. In view of radiocarbon dates for the abandonment of La Venta at around 400 B.C., the Spinden correlation, which would give a date 260 years earlier — 291 B.C., at first glance offers a better fit. However, as Armillas (1964: 304) points out, radiocarbon data from La Venta can be interpreted as showing that the site survived as late as the time of Christ. In view of the GMT correlation's closer agreement with radiocarbon determinations of Long Count Maya monuments, I prefer it to the Spinden. Accepting the GMT correlated 31 B.C. date for Stela C means that we can fix in time the jaguar mask (Fig. 15) on the face opposite that of the date.

The face appears even more evolved than those on the axes uppermost in the sequence of votive axes. It has been incorporated into a rectangular format by the use of straight lines at right angles. This feature should not blind us to the remarkable similarity of the Stela C mask to those flanking the stairs of structure E-VII sub at Uaxactún, Petén, Guatemala (Fig. 15). Upper Preclassic Chicanel pottery was found in the fill of the platform mound. At Tikal a Chicanel tomb yields a radiocarbon date of around A.D. 1 (Thompson 1965: 338). The two masks could be contemporary. In observing their similarities we note that they share identical mouth elements: turned-down lips, a bifid tongue, eye teeth, and fangs curving outward and upward from the upper jaw.

For me, Stela C signals the end of Olmec development. The mask with fangs even more curved than those of the most evolved Olmec axes and the addition of a new element, the bifid tongue, decorates the balustrade of a temple in the Petén jungles. Henceforth, its evolution there may well be Maya evolution. (The Tuxtla Statuette [Fig. 3] with its A.D. 162 date appears to me stylistically more Mayan than Olmec.)

Thus the time of Christ quite possibly marks the end of Olmec style and culture.

What Olmec art can tell us of the socio-political organization of its creators is another aspect of the Olmec problem. As we have stated, the presence of full-time specialists in the arts is obvious. To reach the perfection of Olmec lapidaries and carvers of monoliths would certainly require that one devote all his time to the sculptor's art.

The content of the art reveals religious specialists. For example, in the reliefs from Chalcatzingo (Fig. 11), three personages clad in capes, breechclouts with elaborate belts, and imposing headdresses appear to be holding maize stalks or paddle-like maces as they parade in front of a bound, nude figure with bearded face and erect member. It would be difficult to interpret this scene as other than a fertility ceremony conducted by three priests.

It is assumed that the priests and their retinues were permanent residents in the ceremonial centers of the Olmec heartland. Heizer (1962: 312) presents the reasoning behind this view:

> The religious functionaries shown on the sculptured altars and stelae we may assume to have been masters of formalized ritual, and since these massive carvings represent a high (perhaps the greatest) technical achievement of the society, the priests may be assumed to have occupied a very special and elevated status within that society. Since the La Venta site represents the most substantial evidence of the activity of that society, it may be proposed that the priests held the highest prestige and authority roles in the La Venta population. And from this flows the further indication that the religion which the priests symbolized was a dominant aspect of the society and that this religion served as an integrating or centralizing mechanism with the ceremonial site as its vital center . . . . It is probable that the religion was voluntarily supported by the general population because that same population was beneficiary of the religion.

Most likely the priest-chieftains were the sole patrons of the arts. All Olmec art production seems to have been destined for them; Olmec art is hieratic as contrasted to peasant art. In the Valley of Mexico this separation is dramatically obvious. Olmec art found in the Middle Preclassic horizon existed contemporaneously with the traditional peasant art of Lower Preclassic heritage. Where Olmec art occurs the presence of priest patrons for it can be inferred. Exceptions would be cases where, because of its appeal and prestige value, Olmec art was copied by peasant artists for a peasant clientele.

In depicting the presumed relationship of Maya priests to peasant communities, William Coe (1952: 69) could just as well be describing the dynamics of Olmec priests in contact with "a community with a relatively static, insular, uncomplicated culture, but one that could not mitigate the profound uncertainties of agricultural life. The priestly group, whether foreign or locally derived, appears to have claimed this power and thus was able to extract enormous labor from the countryside — labor that fashioned a context for the power itself."

How far did this theocratic power reach? Monuments in the Olmec style extend from northern Veracruz to Guatemala and El Salvador. Does this mean that Olmec political power could have engulfed the area within these boundaries? Conceivably the introduction of Olmec art to these far reaches could have been carried out by any one of three groups: priest-missionaries, traders, or warriors. M. Coe (1963a: 34) believes that warriors played a decisive role in the dissemination, saying that "not only through diffusion into lesser tribal cultures, but also by means of outright imperialistic invasion of regions as distant as El Salvador, the Olmecs set their stamp upon southeastern Mesoamerica . . . ." Coe's evidence in support of imperialistic invasion is that Olmec figures on reliefs outside the heartland brandish clubs and "knuckle-dusters." But how is one to distinguish between clubs and symbols of authority such as ceremonial maces? That ritual paraphernalia are displayed is indicated by the unmistakable maize stalks held in the same vertical position as the maces and by identically garbed personages on reliefs from Chalcatzingo (Fig. 11) and at Actopan (Fig. 13).

Olmec art lacks representations that can be taken as nothing other than warriors. In the Maya mural paintings of Bonampak, in comparison, personages with shields and spears leave no doubt as to what is being shown. Olmec art displays nothing so definite as to be unequivocally interpreted as arms of conquest.

Proof is thus lacking in support of Olmec imperialism. Since imperialistic invasion is an essential part of the process of empire building, we cannot speak with certainty of an Olmec empire. Only if Olmec priest-rulers had imposed themselves upon their neighbors by military force would an empire have been forged. What Caso (1965) has called an "Olmec presence" is evident over much of Mesoamerica, but, as he adds, it is difficult to explain how this presence diffused. In Europe the "Gothic presence" and the "Roman presence" are equally evident, but they appeared through quite different means.

The Olmec stylistic unity of Mesoamerica in Preclassic times is definite. It reflects an ideological unity if not a political one. Olmec religious ideology seems to lay the groundwork for the Mesoamerican religion of later times: a religion that ignored political borders. It is also possible that it played a similar role in the development of Andean religion. Now, for the first time, we can say with some assurance that the preeminently consequential development of Olmec ideology had its earliest beginnings in the Mixteca Alta of Oaxaca.

Bibliography

Bibliography

ARMILLAS, PEDRO
    1964   Northern Mesoamerica. In *Prehistoric Man in the New World*, edited by Jesse D. Jennings and Edward Norbeck, pp. 291-329. University of Chicago Press, Chicago.

AVELEYRA, ARROYO DE ANDA
    1965   Una nueva cabeza colosal Olmeca. *Boletín del Instituto Nacional de Antropología e Historia*, No. 20, pp. 12-14. Mexico.

BEARDSLEY, RICHARD K. *et. al.*
    1956   Functional and Evolutionary Implications of Community Patterning. In "Seminars in Archaeology: 1955," edited by Robert Wauchope, pp. 131-57. *Memoirs of the Society for American Archaeology*, No. 11. Salt Lake City.

BELTRAN, ALBERTO
    1965   Reportaje gráfico del hallazgo de Las Limas. *Boletín del Instituto Nacional de Antropología e Historia*, No. 21, pp. 9-16. Mexico.

BEYER, HERMANN
  1927   Nota bibliográfica sobre "Tribes and Temples." *El México Antiguo*, Vol. 2, pp. 305-12. Mexico.

BLOM, FRANS AND OLIVER LA FARGE
  1926–27   Tribes and Temples. 2 Vols. *Middle American Research Series, Tulane University, Publication 1*, New Orleans.

BOAS, FRANZ
  1955   *Primitive Art* (originally published 1927). Dover, New York.

BOGGS, STANLEY H.
  1950   Olmec Pictographs in the Las Victorias Group, Chalchuapa Archaeological Zone, El Salvador. *Carnegie Institution of Washington, Division of Historical Research, Notes on Middle American Archaeology and Ethnology*, No. 99. Cambridge.

BRAIDWOOD, ROBERT JOHN AND BRUCE HOWE
  1960   Prehistoric Investigations in Iraqui Kurdistan. *The Oriental Institute of the University of Chicago, Studies in Ancient Oriental Civilization*, No. 31. Chicago.

CARNEIRO, ROBERT L.
  1962   Scale Analysis as an Instrument for the Study of Cultural Evolution. *Southwestern Journal of Anthropology*, Vol. 18, No. 2, pp. 149-169. Albuquerque.

CARNEIRO, ROBERT L. AND STEPHEN F. TOBIAS
  1963   The Application of Scale Analysis to the Study of Cultural Evolution. *Transactions of the New York Academy of Sciences*, Ser. II, Vol. 26, No. 2, pp. 196-207.

CASO, ALFONSO
  1963   Land Tenure Among the Ancient Mexicans. *American Anthropologist*, Vol. 65, No. 4, pp. 863-78. Menasha. (Translated by Charles R. Wicke.)

  1964   Posibilidades de un imperio "olmeca." Unpublished lecture delivered at El Colegio Nacional de Mexico, August 24, 1964. Mexico.

  1965a   ¿Existió un imperio olmeca? *Memorias del Colegio Nacional*, Vol. 3, pp. 11-60. Mexico.

  1965b   Sculpture and Mural Painting of Oaxaca. In *Handbook of Middle American Indians*, edited by Robert Wauchope, Vol. 3, pp. 849-70. University of Texas Press, Austin.

CHAVERO, D. ALFREDO
  1887   *México a través de los siglos*. Mexico and Barcelona.

COE, MICHAEL D.

1957   Cycle 7 Monuments in Middle America: a Reconsideration. *American Anthropologist*, Vol. 59, No. 4, pp. 597-611.

1962   An Olmec Design on an Early Peruvian Vessel. *American Antiquity*, Vol. 27, No. 4. pp. 579-80. Salt Lake City.

1963a Cultural Development in Southern Mesoamerica. In "Aboriginal Cultural Development in Latin America: An Interpretative Review," edited by Betty J. Meggers and Clifford Evans, pp. 27-44. *Smithsonian Miscellaneous Collections*, Vol. 146, No. 1. Washington.

1963b Olmec and Chavín: Rejoinder to Lanning. *American Antiquity*, Vol. 29, No. 1, pp. 101-104. Salt Lake City.

1965a Archaeological Synthesis of Southern Veracruz and Tabasco. In *Handbook of Middle American Indians*, edited by Robert Wauchope, Vol. 3, pp. 679-715. University of Texas Press, Austin.

1965b *The Jaguar's Children: Pre-Classic Central Mexico*. Museum of Primitive Art, New York.

1965c The Olmec Style and its Distribution. In *Handbook of Middle American Indians*, edited by Robert Wauchope, Vol. 3, pp. 739-775. University of Texas Press, Austin.

1966   *Preliminary Report on the First Season's Work at San Lorenzo Tenochtitlan, Veracruz*. Department of Anthropology, Yale University, New Haven.

COE, WILLIAM R.

1959   Piedras Negras Archaeology: Artifacts, Caches and Burials. *University of Pennsylvania, Museum Monographs*.

COVARRUBIAS, MIGUEL

1946   *Mexico South: The Isthmus of Tehuantepec*. Knopf, New York.

1957   *Indian Art of Mexico and Central America*. Knopf, New York.

DRUCKER, PHILIP

1943   Ceramic Sequences at Tres Zapotes, Veracruz, Mexico. *Bureau of American Ethnology, Bulletin* 140. Washington.

1947   Some Implications of the Ceramic Complex of La Venta. *Smithsonian Miscellaneous Collections*, Vol. 107, No. 8. Washington.

1952   La Venta, Tabasco: A Study of Olmec Ceramics and Art. *Bureau of American Ethnology, Bulletin* 153. Washington.

1961   The La Venta Olmec Support Area. *Kroeber Anthropological Society Papers*, No. 25, pp. 59-72. Berkeley.

DRUCKER, PHILIP AND EDUARDO CONTRERAS
    1953   Site Patterns in the Eastern Part of Olmec Territory. *Journal of the Washington Academy of Sciences*, Vol. 43, No. 12, pp. 389-396.

DRUCKER, PHILIP AND ROBERT HEIZER
    1956   Gifts for the Jaguar God. *National Geographic*, Vol. 110, pp. 366-375.
    1960   A Study of the Milpa System of La Venta Island and Its Archaeological Implications. *Southwestern Journal of Anthropology*, Vol. 16, No. 1, pp. 36-45.

DRUCKER, PHILIP, ROBERT F. HEIZER, AND ROBERT J. SQUIER
    1959   Excavations at La Venta, Tabasco, 1955. *Bureau of American Ethnology, Bulletin* 170. Washington.

DURKHEIM, EMILE
    1961   *The Elementary Forms of the Religious Life* (originally published 1912). Collier, New York. (Translated by Joseph Ward Swain.)

EKHOLM, GORDON F.
    1964   Transpacific Contacts. In *Prehistoric Man in the New World*, edited by Jesse D. Jennings and Edward Norbeck, pp. 489-510. University of Chicago Press, Chicago.

FERDON, EDWIN N., JR.
    1953   Tonalá, Mexico. *Monographs of the School of American Research*, 16. Santa Fe.

FISCHER, ERNST
    1963   *The Necessity of Art*. Penguin Books, London.

FISCHER, J. L.
    1961   Art Styles as Cultural Cognitive Maps. *American Anthropologist*, Vol. 63, No. 1, pp. 79-93.

FORSTER, E. M.
    1949   Art for Art's Sake. *Harper's Magazine*, August, pp. 31-34.

FREEMAN, LINTON C. AND ROBERT F. WINCH
    1957   Social Complexity: An Empirical Test of a Typology of Societies. *American Journal of Sociology*, Vol. 62, pp. 461-466.

GAY, CARLO T. E.
    1966   Rock Carvings at Chalcacingo. *Natural History*, Vol. 75, No. 7, pp. 57-61. American Museum of Natural History, New York.
    1967   Oldest Paintings of the New World. *Natural History*, Vol. 76, No. 4, pp. 28-35.

GOODENOUGH, WARD H.

1944   A Technique for Scale Analysis. *Educational and Psychological Measurement*, Vol. 4, pp. 179-190.

1963   Some Applications of Guttman Scale Analysis to Ethnography and Culture Theory. *Southwestern Journal of Anthropology*, Vol. 19, No. 3, pp. 235-250. Albuquerque.

GUTTMAN, LOUIS

1941   The Quantification of a Class of Attributes: A Theory and Method of Scale Construction. In "The Prediction of Personal Adjustment." *Social Sciences Research Council Bulletin*, 48.

1944   A Basis for Scaling Qualitative Data. *American Sociological Review*, Vol. 9, pp. 39-150.

GUZMAN, EULALIA

1934   Los relieves de las rocas del Cerro de la Cantera, Jonacatepec, Morelos. *Anales del Museo Nacional de Arqueología, Historia y Etnología*, 5a época, Vol. 1, No. 2. Mexico.

HARRIS, MARVIN

1959   The Economy Has No Surplus? *American Anthropologist*, Vol. 61, No. 2, pp. 185-199.

HASELBERGER, HERTA

1961   Methods of Studying Ethnological Art. *Current Anthropology*. Vol. 2, No. 4, pp. 341-384.

HAUSER, ARNOLD

1957   *The Social History of Art*, Vol. 1 (originally published 1951). Vintage, New York. (Translated by Stanley Godman.)

1963   *The Philosophy of Art History*. Meridian Books, Cleveland.

HEIZER, R. F.

1960   Agriculture and the Theocratic State in Lowland Southeastern Mexico. *American Antiquity*, Vol. 26, No. 2, pp. 15-22. Menasha.

1961   Inferences on the Nature of Olmec Society Based Upon Data from the La Venta Site. *Kroeber Anthropological Society Papers*, No. 25, pp. 43-58. Berkeley.

1962   The Possible Sociopolitical Structure of the La Venta Olmecs. *Akten des 34 Internationalen Amerkanistenkongresses*, pp. 310-317. Vienna.

HEIZER, R. F. AND H. WILLIAMS

1960   Olmec Lithic Sources. *Boletín Centro de Investigaciones Antropológicas de Mexico*, Vol. 6, pp. 16-17. Mexico.

HOLLAND, WILLIAM
    1961   Relaciones entre la Religión Tzotzil contemporánea y la Maya antigua. *Anales de Instituto Nacional de Antropología e Historia*, Vol. 13, pp. 113-131. Mexico.

    1964   Contemporary Tzotzil Cosmological Concepts as a Basis for Interpreting Prehistoric Maya Civilization. *American Antiquity*, Vol. 29, No. 3, pp. 301-306. Salt Lake City.

HOLMES, W. H.
    1907   On a Nephrite Statuette from San Andres Tuxtla, Vera Cruz, Mexico. *American Anthropologist*, Vol. 9, pp. 691-701. Menasha.

JIMENEZ MORENO, WIGBERTO
    1942   El enigma de los olmecas. *Cuadernos Americanos*, Año 1, No. 5. Mexico.

    1957   Síntesis de la Historia Pretolteca de Mesoamérica. In *Esplendor del México Antiguo*, edited by Carmen Cook de Leonard, Vol. 2, pp. 1019-1108. Centro de Investigaciones Antropológicas de México, México. In English: 1966, Mesoamerica Before the Toltecs. In *Ancient Oaxaca*, edited by John Paddock, pp. 3-82. Stanford University Press, Stanford. (Trans. Maudie Bullington and Charles R. Wicke.)

JOYCE, THOMAS A. AND H. A. KNOX
    1931   Sculptured Figures from Vera Cruz State, Mexico. *Man*, Vol. 31, No. 19. London.

KAPLAN, DAVID
    1963   Men, Monuments, and Political Systems. *Southwestern Journal of Anthropology*, Vol. 19, No. 4, pp. 397-410. Albuquerque.

KELEMAN, PAL
    1961   *Medieval American Art*. 2 vols. New York.

KELLEY, DAVID H.
    1962   Glyphic Evidence for a Dynastic Sequence at Quiriguá, Guatemala. *American Antiquity*, Vol. 27, No. 3, pp. 323-335. Salt Lake City.

KIDDER, ALFRED II
    1964   South American High Cultures, In *Prehistoric Man in the New World*, edited by Jessie D. Jennings and Edward Norbeck, pp. 451-486. University of Chicago Press, Chicago.

Köhler, W.
    1963   Gestalt Psychology. In "History of Psychology," Vol. 18, pp. 715-717. *Encyclopaedia Britannica*. Chicago.

Kroeber, A. L.
    1948   *Anthropology*. Harcourt, Brace & World, New York and Burlingame.
    1957   *Style and Civilizations*. Cornell University Press, Ithaca.

Kroeber, A. L. and Clyde Kluckhohn
    1961   *Culture: A Critical Review of Concepts and Definitions*. Vintage, New York.

Kubler, George
    1962a   *The Art and Architecture of Ancient America*. Penguin Books, Baltimore.
    1962b   *The Shape of Time*. Yale University Press, New Haven.

Lathrop, Donald W.
    1964   Review of *The Art and Architecture of Ancient America* by George Kubler. *American Antiquity*, Vol. 29, No. 3, pp. 398-399.

Lehmann, Walter
    1926   Reisebrief aus Puerto Mexico. *Zeitschrift für Ethnologie*, Jahrg. 1926, pp. 171-177. Berlin.

Lewis, Phillip H.
    1961   A Definition of Primitive Art. *Fieldiana Anthropology, Chicago Natural History Museum*, Vol. 36, No. 10. Chicago.

MacNeish, Richard S.
    1964   The Origins of New World Civilization. *Scientific American*, Vol. 211, No. 5.

Marti, Samuel
    1965a   ¿Ciudad perdida de los mixtecos? Nueva zona arqueológica en la Mixteca Alta: Acropolis de las ruinas de Diquiyú, Oaxaca. *Cuardernos Americanos*, Vol. 24, No. 1, Mexico.
    1965b   Diquiyú: Un señorío zapoteco-mixteco ignoto. *Cuardernos Americanos*, Vol. 24, No. 2, Mexico.
    1965c   Un ignoto señorío en la Mixteca Alta, Oaxaca: Diquiyú. In "México en la Cultura," *Novedades* 16 May, Mexico.

MEDELLIN ZENIL, ALFONSO
    1960   Monolitos Inéditos Olmecas. *La Palabra y el Hombre, Revista de la Universidad Veracruzana*, 16, pp. 75-97. Jalapa.
    1965   La Escultura de las Limas. *Boletín del Instituto Nacional de Antropología e Historia*, No. 21, pp. 5-9. Mexico.

MELGAR Y SERRANO, JOSE MARIA
    1871   Estudio sobre la antigüidad y el origen de la Cabeza Colosal de tipo etiópico que existe en Hueyapan. *Boletín Sociedad Mexicana de Geografía y Estadística*, 2 época, Vol. 2, pp. 104-109. Mexico.

MILES, S. W.
    1965   Sculpture of the Guatemala-Chiapas Highlands and Pacific Slopes. In *Handbook of Middle American Indians*, edited by Robert Wauchope, Vol. 2, pp. 237-275. University of Texas Press, Austin.

MILLS, C. WRIGHT
    1959   *The Power Elite*. Oxford University Press, New York.

MORLEY, S. G.
    1946   *The Ancient Maya*. Stanford University Press, Palo Alto.

MUNRO, THOMAS
    1949   *The Arts and Their Interrelations*. The Liberal Arts Press, New York.
    1963   *Evolution in the Arts*. The Cleveland Museum of Art, Cleveland.

New York Times
    1957   Obituary of Miguel Covarrubias, Feb. 6, p. 26.

PADDOCK, JOHN
    1966   Oaxaca in Ancient Mesoamerica. In *Ancient Oaxaca*, edited by John Paddock, pp. 83-242. Stanford University Press, Stanford.

PANOFSKY, ERWIN
    1955   *Meaning in the Visual Arts*. Doubleday, Garden City.

PIÑA CHAN, ROMAN
    1955   *Las Culturas Preclásicas de la Cuenca de México*. Fondo de Cultura Económica, Mexico.

PINART, ALPHONSE
    1885   Opinion au sujet des Olmèques. Société de Géographie de Paris. *Comptes Rendus*, p. 586.

PORTER, MURIEL
    1953   Tlatilco and the Pre-Classic Cultures of the New World. *Viking Fund, Publication* 19. New York.

PROSKOURIAKOFF, TATIANA
    1950   A Study of Classic Maya Sculpture. *Carnegie Institution of Washington, Publication* 593. Washington.

    1953   Scroll Patterns *(entrelaces)* of Veracruz. In *Huastecos, Totonacos y sus Vecinos*, edited by Ignacio Bernal and Eusebio Dávalos Hurtado, pp. 389-401. Sociedad Mexicana de Antropología, Mexico.

    1960   Historical Implications of a Pattern of Dates at Piedras Negras, Guatemala. *American Antiquity*, Vol. 25, No. 4, pp. 454-475. Salt Lake City.

    1963   Review of *The Art and Architecture of Ancient America* by George Kubler. *American Journal of Archaeology*, Vol. 67, No. 3, pp. 323-24. Princeton.

REDFIELD, ROBERT
    1941   *The Folk Culture of Yucatan*. University of Chicago Press, Chicago.

    1953   *The Primitive World and Its Transformation*. Cornell University Press, Ithaca.

RICHARDSON, JANE AND A. L. KROEBER
    1940   Three Centuries of Women's Dress Fashions; A Quantitative Analysis. *Anthropological Records*, Vol. 5, pp. 111-153. Berkeley and Los Angeles.

SAHAGUN, BERNARDINO DE
    1961   *General History of the Things of New Spain; Florentine Codex*, Vol. 10. Translated by Arthur J. O. Anderson and Charles E. Dibble, School of American Research, Santa Fe.

SANDERS, WILLIAM T.
    1963   Review of *Mexico* by Michael D. Coe. *American Anthropologist*, Vol. 65, No. 4, pp. 972-973.

SAVILLE, MARSHALL H.
    1929   Votive Axes from Ancient Mexico. *Indian Notes, Museum of the American Indian, Heye Foundation*, Vol. 6, No. 4, pp. 335-342. New York.

SELER, EDUARD
    1906   Die Monumente von Hiulocintla im Canton Tuxpan des Staates
            Vera Cruz. *Compte rendu de la XV éme Session du Congrés
            International des Americanistes*. [Quebec 1906], Vol. 2, pp.
            381-387.

SELER-SACHS, (FRAU) CECILE
    1922   Altertümer des Kanton Tuxtla im Staate Vera Cruz. *Festschrift
            Eduard Seler*, pp. 543-556. Stuttgart.

SMITH, TILLIE
    1963   The Main Themes of the "Olmec" Art Tradition. *Kroeber
            Anthropological Society Papers*, No. 28, pp. 121-123. Berkeley.

SOROKIN, PITIRIM
    1928   *Contemporary Sociological Theories*. Harper and Brothers, New
            York.
    1962   *Social and Cultural Dynamics*. 4 vols. Bedminster Press, New
            York.

STEWARD, JULIAN H.
    1955   *Theory of Culture Change*. University of Illinois Press, Urbana.

STIRLING, M. W.
    1939   Discovering the New World's Oldest Dated Work of Man.
            National Geographic, Vol. 76, pp. 183-218.
    1941   Expedition Unearths Buried Masterpieces of Carved Jade. *National Geographic*, Vol. 80, pp. 277-302.
    1943a   Stone Monuments of Southern Mexico. *Bureau of American
            Ethnology, Bulletin* 140. Washington.
    1943b   La Venta's Green Stone Tigers. *National Geographic*, Vol. 84,
            pp. 321-332.
    1947   On the Trail of La Venta Man. *National Geographic*, Vol. 91,
            pp. 137-172.
    1965   Monumental Sculpture of Southern Veracruz and Tabasco. In
            Handbook of Middle American Indians, edited by Robert Wauchope, Vol. 3, pp. 716-738. University of Texas Press, Austin.

STIRLING, M. W. AND MARION STIRLING
    1942   Finding Jewels of Jade in a Mexican Swamp. *National Geographic*, Vol. 82, pp. 635-661.

THOMPSON, J. ERIC S.

1941   Dating of Certain Inscriptions of Non-Maya Origin. *Carnegie Institution of Washington, Division of Historical Research, Theoretical Approaches to Problems*, No. 1. Cambridge.

1943   Some Sculptures from Southeastern Quetzaltenango, Guatemala. *Carnegie Institution of Washington, Division of Historical Research, Middle American Archaeology and Ethnology*, No. 17. Cambridge.

1954   *The Rise and Fall of Maya Civilization*. University of Oklahoma Press, Norman.

1965   Archaeological Synthesis of the Southern Maya Lowlands. In *Handbook of Middle American Indians*, edited by Robert Wauchope, Vol. 2, pp. 331-359. University of Texas Press, Austin.

VAILLANT, GEORGE C.

1932   A Precolumbian Jade. *Natural History*, Vol. 32, pp. 512-520. American Museum of Natural History, New York.

VEBLEN, THORSTEIN

1899   *The Theory of the Leisure Class*. Macmillan, New York.

WATERMAN, T. T.

1924   On Certain Antiquities in Western Guatemala. *Bulletin of the Pan American Union*. Washington.

1929   Is the Baul Stela an Aztec Imitation? *Art and Archaeology*, Vol. 28, pp. 182-187. Washington.

WAUCHOPE, ROBERT

1950   A Tentative Sequence of Pre-Classic Ceramics in Middle America. *Tulane University, Middle American Research Records*, Vol. 1, No. 14. New Orleans.

1954   Implications of Radiocarbon Dates from Middle and South America. *Tulane University, Middle American Research Records*, Vol. 2, Nos. 1-8. New Orleans.

1964   Southern Mesoamerica. In *Prehistoric Man in the New World*, edited by Jesse D. Jennings and Edward Norbeck, pp. 331-386. University of Chicago Press, Chicago.

WEIANT, C. W.

1943   An Introduction to the Ceramics of Tres Zapotes, Veracruz, Mexico. *Bureau of American Ethnology Bulletin* 139. Washington.

1952   Reply to "Middle Tres Zapotes and the Preclassic Ceramic Sequence," *American Antiquity*, Vol. 18, No. 1, pp. 57-59.

WEYERSTALL, A.

1932   Some Observations on Indian Mounds, Idols, and Pottery in the Low Papaloapan Basin, State of Vera Cruz, Mexico. *Tulane University, Middle American Research Papers*, No. 4, pp. 23-69. New Orleans.

WILLEY, GORDON R.

1962   The Early Great Styles and the Rise of the Pre-Columbian Civilizations. *American Anthropologist*, Vol. 64, No. 1, Pt. 1, pp. 1-14. Menasha.

WOLF, E. R.

1959   *Sons of the Shaking Earth*. University of Chicago Press, Chicago.

Index

Index